Iterative Optimizers

Difficulties increase the nearer we get to the goal.
– Johann Wolfgang von Goethe

There are much less difficulties in solving a problem than in defining it.
– Joseph de Maistre

Iterative Optimizers

Difficulty Measures and Benchmarks

Maurice Clerc

WILEY

First published 2019 in Great Britain and the United States by ISTE Ltd and John Wiley & Sons, Inc.

ISTE Ltd
27-37 St George's Road
London SW19 4EU
UK

www.iste.co.uk

John Wiley & Sons, Inc.
111 River Street
Hoboken, NJ 07030
USA

www.wiley.com

Library of Congress Control Number: 2019930133

British Library Cataloguing-in-Publication Data
A CIP record for this book is available from the British Library
ISBN 978-1-78630-409-4

Contents

Preface

The Essentials

– Problems in a set of test cases can be classified according to several difficulty measures consistent with one another, in other words approximately giving the same ordering relation;

– these measures are valid for optimizers that explicitly or implicitly assume that "nearer is better", in probability;

– some can be estimated using the Monte Carlo method, when the structure of the landscapes of the problems of the test case is unknown (basins of attraction, plateaus, local minima). Computations, however, can take a very long time;

– one of the measures presented requires an acceptable error threshold to be assumed, but its coding only takes a few lines. The other measure, somewhat more complex because it is based on position triplets, does not require an error threshold to be *a priori* defined, but is less reliable in the presence of plateaus;

– another difficulty indicator, δ_0, is proposed based on the structure of the landscape of the problem. It is consistent with previous ones and can be quickly calculated, but it requires the basins of attraction and plateaus of the problem landscape to be known;

– since this information is rarely given and difficult to find in conventional test cases, the LandGener program is specifically designed to create known structure landscapes, upon which δ_0 is easily computable;

– a typology of all possible landscapes is established, essentially in terms of modality and plateau ratio, with the estimate of the relative significance of each class;

– some conventional test cases are analyzed based on this typology. It is shown that they are biased in favor of certain types of problems, for example, unimodal ones or ones without plateaus. However, the application of a difficulty measure makes it possible to classify their problems, from the easiest to the more selective;

– rigorous definitions of the concepts of usage and exploration are given, making them measurable. The main types of evolution of their ratio (balance profiles) are studied.

Maurice CLERC
January 2019

Introduction

Every year, not to say every month, a new optimization algorithm is proposed, accompanied by the creator's claim that it is superior to the previous ones. This type of assertion is based on test results achieved with test cases, more specifically a selection of problems to which the algorithm is applied.

In *Guided Randomness in Optimization* (Clerc 2015), I show that it is easy to choose a set of test cases and the way the results are addressed to seemingly "justify" this superiority.

For example, consider the test case of Table I.1, which was actually used in an article[1]. With such a set of problems, an algorithm has to be defined whose signature (see section A.3) is biased in favor of the center of the search space to obtain good results. At the extreme, if the algorithm is to be seen as a black box inside of which the test case is introduced and that offers a solution, there is a "magical" box that finds the perfect solution of each of the functions in a time almost equal to zero[2].

---

1 I do not provide the reference because it does not seem useful to increase the number of citations. Note though that some very similar ones have also been published.

2 The algorithm contained in the box is simply:

– evaluate the point $(0, 0, \ldots, 0)$;

– evaluate the point $(1, 1, \ldots, 1)$;

– propose the best of both as a solution.

Name	Equation
Sphere	$\sum_{d=1}^{D} x_d^2$
Rosenbrock	$\sum_{d=1}^{D-1} \left(100 \left(x_d^2 - x_{d+1} \right)^2 + (1 - x_d)^2 \right)$
Ellipsoid	$\sum_{d=1}^{D} \left(|x_d| + 0,5 \right)^2$
Rastrigin	$\sum_{d=1}^{D} \left(x_d^2 - 10 \cos \left(2\pi x_d \right) + 10 \right)$
Ackley	$-20 e^{-0,2 \sqrt{\frac{1}{n} \sum_{d=1}^{D} x_d^2}} - e^{\frac{1}{n} \sum_{d=1}^{D} \cos(2\pi x_d)} + 20 + e$

Table I.1. *A biased test case in a published article (see footnote 1). The names of the functions have been kept*

Obviously, if users, impressed by the optimistic conclusions of the presentation of the algorithm, try to apply it to their own problems, they will almost surely get very bad results.

This lack of reliability is due to the fact that the test set is not representative of the problems that the user will have to solve.

Moreover, in practice, it is interesting that a test case contains problems of different levels of difficulty. In fact, this allows a better hierarchization of the algorithms tested with this test case, knowing that users will not necessarily prefer the algorithm capable of solving most difficult problems if theirs are not so much and that in addition, this algorithm is very expensive in terms of computing resources. A precise definition of the term "difficulty" is therefore necessary. This is far from being trivial, because, as shown in the small example above, the difficulty of an optimization depends on the optimizer being used.

Therefore, after reading this book, you should be able, in principle:

– to analyze the structure of a set of test cases and to deduce therefrom which types of optimizers it promotes;

– to build your own set of test cases, with given characteristics (class of optimizers under consideration, levels of difficulty);

– to perform a well-based critical assessment on optimizers presented in the literature.

Reading guide

This book, short but dense (beware!), is actually a collection of studies related to the question "How can optimizers be reliably compared?". As such, chapters can be read almost independently of each other. It is, however, advisable to start with the chapter of definitions, some not being completely conventional.

Based on your knowledge of the subject and your areas of interest, it is thus possible, for example, to directly consult Chapter 6, even if, for the very last section, it is necessary to have previously studied a difficulty measure presented in Chapter 2.

Similarly, if you are a practitioner especially curious to see how "customized" landscapes can be created, Chapter 4 on the LandGener program is right for you. On the contrary, the chapter on the typology of landscapes (Chapter 3), full of mathematical formulas, may appear to be rather boring and one could just browse the conclusions, or even ignore it completely.

And, of course, the various sections of the appendix are even more independent and non-essential, despite the fact that they can provide useful information, such as examples of deceptive functions and small codes sources. Regarding the latter, in fact, it should be noted that the main ones are not given here but may be downloaded (see www.iste.co.uk/clerc/iterative.zip).

More comprehensively, here are some observations on each chapter (Excluding the Appendix):

– Chapter 1: "Some definitions". The most important ones are those concerning basins, plateaus and structures, but if readers intend to avoid Chapter 3, it is alternatively possible, as a first step, to skip this chapter and to merely consider intuitive notions.

– Chapter 2: "Difficulty of the difficulty". The difficulty measures that will then be used almost everywhere are defined here. This is therefore a chapter to be almost necessarily read.

– Chapter 3: Landscape typology". One to be skipped if the reader is allergic to combinatorial computations. Nonetheless, it might prove useful to take a look at the findings.

– Chapter 4: "LandGener". It is essentially the presentation of principles allowing for the "customized" creation of landscapes – and, therefore, of test cases – with a few examples.

– Chapter 5: "Test cases". Critical analysis of two sets of conventional test cases. It is made according to the typology seen in Chapter 3, but it is not really necessary to have read the latter if the reader trusts its conclusions!

– Chapter 6: "Difficulty vs dimension". A small study around the notion, not always correct, that the difficulty increases with the dimension (the number of variables) of the problem.

– Chapter 7: "Exploitation and exploration vs difficulty". In fact, this chapter and the next one form a whole. Exploitation and exploration concepts, often merely qualitative, are formally defined and measurable. The possible evolutions of their ratios (balance profiles) are studied.

– Chapter 8: "The Explo2 algorithm". As an example, it is shown that it is possible to write a small optimizer explicitly using a predefined balance profile and that it is relatively effective despite being greedy in computational time. This is probably the chapter most likely to incur successful developments.

– Chapter 9: "Balance and perceived difficulty". Slightly heterogeneous, but the two experimental studies that it contains are too short to justify specific chapters. One concerns the impact of the profile balance on performance, and the other makes it possible to insist on the fact that a difficulty measure only gives an ordering relation on a set of problems, without prejudice to quantitative differences between the difficulties actually collected by a given optimizer.

1

Some Definitions

An important point is that one is supposed to work with a digital computer and that, consequently, every manipulated entity is discrete finite. In particular, the difference between two values cannot be less than a given threshold ε, commonly known as computer machine epsilon, even if, in fact, it also depends on the operating system and the language being used.

Most theoretical analyses, especially for convergences, require continuity or even differentiability properties. As a result, they are not valid in our discrete context. A convergence theorem may very simply not hold therein.

1.1. Continuous case vs discrete case: when a theorem no longer holds

A classical theorem is when, with the set of non-negative real numbers, the sequence $x_{n+1} = \alpha x_n$ converges to zero for every α positive smaller than 1, and this holds independently of the initial number x_1.

However, on a computer, this is different. For simplicity, suppose a machine epsilon ε equal to 1. Then, αx_n is rounded to the nearest integer. If, for example, $x_1 = 10$, then the sequence stabilizes at 1 and does not converge to zero. The theorem no longer holds. More specifically, it must be modified: the convergence still exists, but to ε.

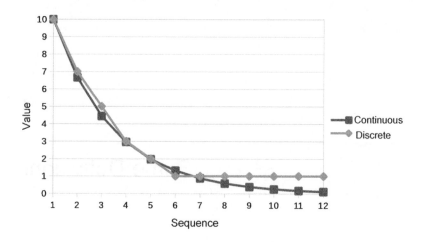

Figure 1.1. *On a digital computer a sequence that theoretically converges to zero may in fact converge to a positive value wrongly said to be zero*

Naturally, this is a simplistic example; however, it encourages considering with much caution any theorem based on an assumption of continuity or, *a fortiori*, of differentiability.

Similarly, one also must consider with suspicion any computational result on digital computer whose absolute value is much smaller than ε. For example, if $\varepsilon = 10^{-32}$, then it cannot be advanced that a statement like the one below is relevant:

With this problem, optimizer A is better than optimizer B, because it yields a minimum equal to 10^{-40} and B only 10^{-35}.

Therefore, although the concepts of iterative optimization are supposedly known (more details are given in Clerc (2015)), it is necessary to partially redefine them, in order to then allow valid analyses, generally based on enumerations.

1.2. Landscape

An optimization problem is defined by a space of points x, known as definition space or search space, valued by a function f. Formally, it is a scalar field, but we are conventionally referring to a *landscape* and the role of an optimizer is to find optimal value point(s). Only the search for minima is considered here (see definition below), as a specific case that can always be easily referred to.

1.2.1. *Size of a landscape*

One might assume that a difficulty measure perceived by an optimizer (see section 2.8) for a given problem must be, among other things, an increasing function of the "size" of the latter. But can we define it?

A simple notion, not to say simplistic, is to say that it is the amount of data needed to describe the landscape of the problem. For example, on a computer which, because of its machine epsilon, can discriminate only N values, a landscape whose point space is of dimension D then has a size

$$T = N^D \qquad\qquad [1.1]$$

In fact, the definition space includes N^D points that can be presumably assumed to be classified, for example, in a lexicographic manner, and the landscape is then completely described by the ordered list of values at each point.

This is not very discriminating, since it implies that for a given D, all landscapes have the same size. In reality, it is a maximal size that assumes that the value at a point is independent of the values at other points. This is true, for example, for a totally random landscape, but does not hold in general. Most fortunately, the only method to find the optimum would otherwise be an exhaustive search. Moreover, the existence of data compression algorithms (of images, for example) effectively shows that it is often possible to do better. See also problems such as that of the traveling salesman with D cities, which can be described using only $D\left(D-1\right)/2$ arc values.

A second idea would be to consider instead the minimum number of values needed to describe the landscape. However, on the one hand, it is often unknown and, on the other hand, it can be in any way related to the difficulty perceived by an optimizer (think of some complex landscapes completely described using simple formulas).

In short, in the absence of a satisfactory definition, we shall simply retain the following: the size is finite and the number of possible landscapes is also finite (one does not imply the other). More precisely, there are N^{N^D} possible landscapes[1]. A consequence is that the requirements of the No Free Lunch Theorem (NFLT) (Wolpert 1997) are satisfied. Thus, on average, all optimizers – including pure random search – are equivalent, however, only on the condition that *every* landscape is really considered. In practice, this is never the case in test cases. Hence, there are two remarks:

– in some published articles, we sometimes see a comment such as "our new algorithm outperforms others with most problems of test cases, but not all, because of the NFLT". This is incorrect. Given that the test case is not exhaustive, nothing prevents in theory that there is an unsurpassable algorithm with this set of problems;

– because each one is incomplete, every test case is necessarily biased, in the sense that they promote such and such types of optimizers. At the least, we could try to build them to be sufficiently representative of certain classes of landscapes of real problems so that they make it possible to usefully discriminate from generalist optimizers. This is precisely one of the subjects of this little book.

1.2.2. *Adjacency and path*

We consider two points $x = (x_1, \ldots, x_D)$ and $y = (y_1, \ldots, y_D)$ of the search space. They are said to be *adjacent* if

$$\max_d \left(|y_d - x_d| \right) = \varepsilon \qquad [1.2]$$

---

1 Therefrom, we could carry out a study of the landscape in terms of information theory, but this would be in a different discussion.

They are thus as close as possible, because of machine epsilon. In fact, equation [1.2] implies that the components of the vector $y - x$ have only three possible values: ε, $-\varepsilon$ and 0.

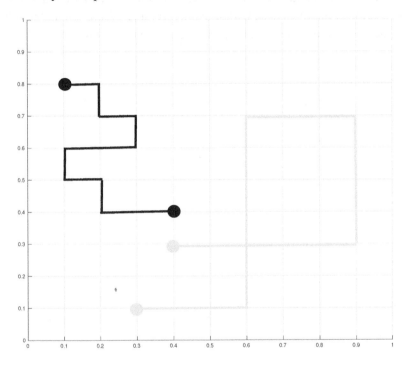

Figure 1.2. *Path examples*

To simplify, instead of saying "points adjacent to", one could say "the adjacents to".

A *path* is a sequence of adjacents.

1.2.3. *Minimum*

A point is a minimum if its value is less than or equal to the values of all its adjacents. If there is no equality, then it is a strict minimum.

A minimum is said to be global if its value is less than or equal to the values of all other minima (and thus, ultimately, of all other points in the definition space). Otherwise, this is a local minimum.

1.2.4. *Modality*

This is the number of local or global minima. We will see that this is a criterion sometimes used to define the difficulty of a problem, but it is in fact much too basic, as intuitively illustrated by Figure 1.3.

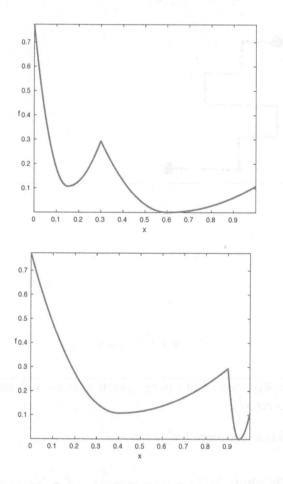

Figure 1.3. *Same modality, but for all classic optimizers the landscape at the bottom is more difficult*

1.2.5. *Plateau*

Let P be a set of points of the search space such that:

– every point of P has the same value v;

– every point of P has at least D adjacents also in P (connexity condition).

Then, P is said to be a plateau of value v. If it is necessary to be more precise, it will sometimes be referred to as D-plateau. Note that a plateau can be seen as a set of minima.

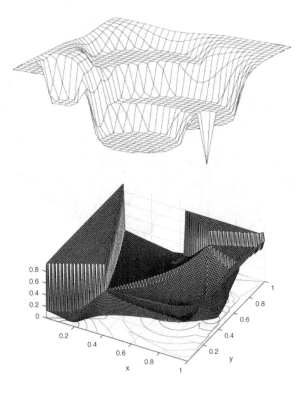

Figure 1.4. *Examples of landscapes with plateaus. The one at the bottom was built with the program LandGener (see Chapter 4). For a color version of this image, see www.iste.co.uk/clerc/iterative.zip*

1.2.6. *Basin of attraction*

Consider a minimum x^* of a landscape f of dimension D. Intuitively, it would be tempting to say that a point x belongs to the basin of attraction of x^* if the following two conditions are met:

– $f(x) > f(x^*)$;

– there exists a path $(x_1 = x, \ldots, x_k, \ldots, x_K = x^*)$ with $f(x_{k+1}) < f(x)$.

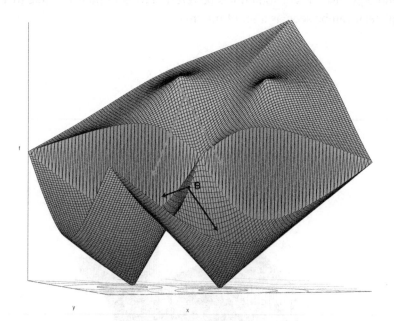

Figure 1.5. *Landscape formed of two basins of attraction. Without the "maximal descent" condition, a point such as A may belong to two basins. With this condition, this may still be the case for a point such as B, at the shared boundary of the basins, but this will not affect the evaluation of the sizes of these basins. For a color version of this image, see www.iste.co.uk/clerc/iterative.zip*

Informally, it can be said that there is a strictly descending path from x to x^*. However, this definition is not precise enough because it allows too easily that a point can be in two basins of attraction (see Figure 1.5).

Rather than the simple "descending" condition, we should instead speak of "maximal descent". The following condition is then added:

– for any k and for any x' adjacent to x_k, different from x_{k+1} and such that $f(x') < f(x_k)$, we have $f(x_k) - f(x_{k+1}) > f(x_k) - f(x')$.

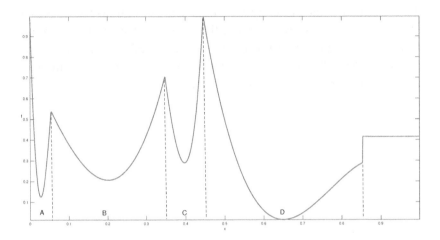

Figure 1.6. $D = 1$. *Four basins of attraction and a plateau*

Since positions are nodes of a grid with similar step in every direction, it is simply a maximum discrete gradient condition. With this more precise definition, it may still happen that a point belongs to two basins, but in practice much more rarely, for example, if it is on their common boundary, which is not a problem when it comes to calculating the sizes of basins. The 1D or 2D analogy underlying this definition is that if the landscape is immersed inside a vertical gravitational field, then a ball placed in x will spontaneously move to x^*.

A slight inconvenience still remains in dimension 1, due to the fact that we are working with discrete finite spaces: any non-surjective monotonic function necessarily comprises one or several plateaus composed of at least two points, which should strictly be considered as many subdomains. In practice, however, micro-plateaus comprising small numbers of points are often overlooked, "as if" they were strictly monotonic landscape portions.

In fact, as we shall see, the basins of attraction play a crucial role in the evaluation of the difficulty for a large class of optimizers, by means of their sizes and also by means of the relative values of their minima. Note that a landscape formed of a plateau and of one or several ascending "sides" is not a single "flat bottom" basin, but the reunion of this plateau with several basins (Figure 1.7).

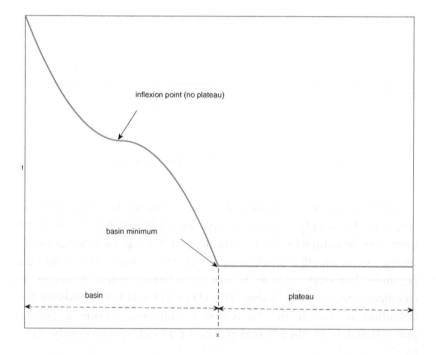

Figure 1.7. *This is not a "flat-bottom" basin, but the union of a plateau and the basin of attraction of the minimum of the basin, which is also one of the minima of the plateau (all of equal value, naturally)*

1.2.7. *Domain*

In order to unify descriptions, the definition space of a landscape can also be called a *domain*. Landscape basins and plateaus are also defined on subdomains. We shall see that to study a landscape, it is rather convenient to consider that all subdomains are D-triangles, namely $D + 1$-vertex polyhedra. In dimension 1, these are of course intervals, classic triangles in dimension 2, tetrahedra in dimension 3 and so on.

For example, as illustrated in Figure 1.8, any D-plateau is defined from a reunion of D-triangles, for example, using the Delaunay method, in which case, it is very generally unique, unless $D + 2$ points are concyclic. Even if there is no uniqueness, the impact on the assessment of the difficulty, when it is essentially based on the value and size of the plateau, is minimal.

The LandGener algorithm, presented in Chapter 4, makes it possible to define a large variety of landscapes based on such decompositions in D-triangles. It however becomes unusable, in terms of computation time, as soon as the dimension increases too much. We shall see then that we can simply make use of D-square[2] decompositions, but at the cost of a drastic reduction in the types of possible landscapes. Nonetheless, this is not a significant disadvantage when we just want to create a series of landscapes of increasing difficulties, for purposes of comparison tests of the effectiveness of different algorithms.

1.2.8. *Structure*

The structure of a landscape is defined by its subdomains, in nature (basin, plateau), value (minimum for a basin, plateau value), size and position (location of the minimum for a basin or of the center of gravity for a plateau).

---

2 Or D-cube; any of the denominations will be used subsequently depending on the context.

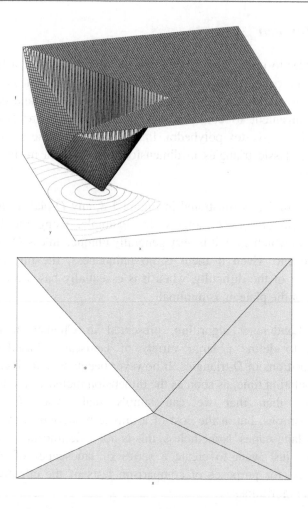

Figure 1.8. *Any plateau support may be broken down into triangles. Using the Delaunay method, the decomposition is generally unique. For a color version of this image, see www.iste.co.uk/clerc/iterative.zip*

It can be said that two landscapes have the same structure according to several precision levels:

– level 1: same number of basins and same number of plateaus;

– level 2: in addition, the sizes of subdomains (basins, plateaus) should be equal;

– level 3: in addition, the minimum values for basins and plateau values must be the same;

– level 4: in addition, the relative positions of minima and centers of gravity of plateaus must be the same.

As already indicated and unless stated otherwise, all landscapes whose definition domain is of dimension D are supposed to be normalized on $[0, 1]^D$. Hence, among other things, in fact, every unimodal landscape of zero minimum has the same structure at level 3 (but not at level 4, in general, because the position of the minimum can be different from one landscape to another).

It should be noted that even descending to level 4, it is seldom that the structure completely defines the landscape and, as a result, any estimate of its difficulty from this structure is more or less associated with uncertainty, *a fortiori* when merely considering level 1 or 2. In this case, for example, the claim that "The more local minima a landscape has, the more difficult it is" does not always hold and it is fairly easy to find counterexamples (see Chapter 6).

2

Difficulty of the Difficulty

It is difficult to define the difficulty of a problem! We shall do it first in an informal manner:

DEFINITION 2.1.– For a given optimizer, the difficulty of a problem is the effort to find an acceptable solution.

We must now give rigorous meaning, namely quantifiable in this case, to the terms *effort* and *acceptable solution.*

2.1. Effort and budgets

Since in practice the optimizers concerned here are computer programs, a simple idea is to consider the computing resources that have been employed, processor time in particular. Storage spaces could also be taken into account, but this is increasingly less a limitation.

However, this measure depends on the computer, on the operating system, on the language in which the code was written and even on the somewhat clever way in which the algorithm was coded. From one researcher to another, results are thus not always reproducible.

Hence, I shall take here another measure, all the more conventional: the number of evaluations made in the search space. Then, the budget will be the maximum number of evaluations allowed. We shall distinguish the partial budget for a single optimizer execution and the total budget, which can be dedicated to optimization. The latter is thus generally the sum of several partial budgets, not necessarily all equal (Clerc 2015).

It should be noted that, depending on algorithms, the effort is not necessarily equal to the number of sampled points, for several reasons:

– a point can be selected to guide the search without having to be evaluated, for example a center of gravity, or because it is outside the landscape definition space;

– a point can be evaluated several times if the optimizer reselects it, having "forgotten" that it has already been used.

For its part, this measure gives reproducible results in various computing environments. It remains far from perfect because it does not take into account the necessary storage space, which is a lesser evil, but above all ancillary computations such as, for example, the occasional use of a surrogate function.

However, the evaluation of a position by a surrogate function is supposed to be significantly faster than the actual evaluation of this position. More generally, it will then be assumed that the cost of this latter is far greater than the computations that led to selecting the position being considered. It is also the case in numerous real problems where an evaluation is actually the execution of a sophisticated model of an industrial process or even of the process itself.

Finally, even though through experiments I could only test a restricted number of optimizers, it seems that for a given optimizer, the ratio of computational times for evaluations, on the one hand, and additional computations, on the other hand, is relatively constant and independent of the problem being addressed. Finally, our quantifiable definition will thus be simply:

DEFINITION 2.2.– Effort = number of evaluations.

2.2. Acceptable solution

For the interested reader, a detailed study of the relationships between effort and result is given in Clerc (2015). Here, I shall merely make use of a terminology from precision mechanics, according to which a *tolerance threshold* (or threshold of acceptability) is a numeric value not to be exceeded. As a first step, we can consider the following definition:

DEFINITION 2.3.– An acceptable solution is a position in the search space whose value is below the tolerance threshold.

Note that this is here what might be called a "tolerance in f" on the values of the function describing the landscape. This is the practitioner's point of view. That of the theorist could be a "tolerance in x", which involves the distance between the proposed solution and the position of a global minimum. The second notion is more restrictive than the first. For example, consider the landscape of Figure 2.1. As soon as the tolerance in f, which we may denote by ϵ_f, is greater than 0.15, it becomes much easier to find a satisfactory solution, since points around the local minimum become acceptable.

We execute N times a stochastic optimizer with a given effort. The number of tests that have passed (for which the value of the solution found is smaller than ϵ_f) is n and the success rate $\tau = \frac{n}{N}$. Therefore, if we draw the curve τ versus ϵ_f, then a discontinuity as seen in Figure 2.2 is obtained.

REMARK 2.1.– With some classic test functions (for example Griewank, see section 6.2), increasing the number of dimensions increases even faster the number of local minima whose values are close to the values of the global minimum. In the end, the problem is then made easier, when considering, as often, only the tolerance in f (see Chapter 6).

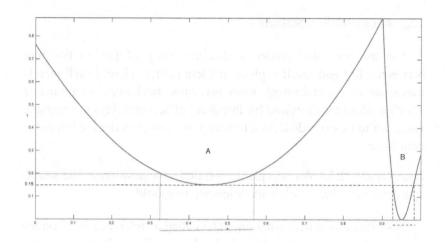

Figure 2.1. *Tolerances in x and f*

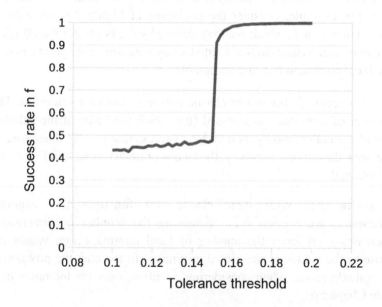

Figure 2.2. *Success rate tolerance in f. When the tolerance makes it possible to accept a local minimum, the success rate sharply increases*

REMARK 2.2.– The criterion of the success rate should be manipulated with great caution. Indeed, in general, it becomes "stable" only after a number of trials well above what is usually done. Consider, for example, Figure 2.3, achieved with the APS algorithm (Omran and Clerc 2016, APS) and a population of six agents on the landscape of Figure 2.1. For an effort of 70 evaluations, performing 100 tests only results in displaying a 69% optimistic success rate. In fact, with 1,000 and mainly 10,000 tests, it can be seen that it is rather about 60%.

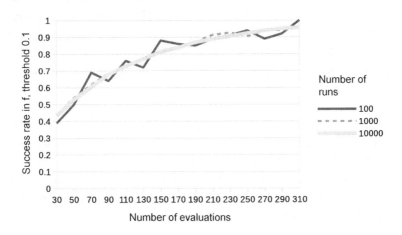

Figure 2.3. *Success rate vs number of evaluations. Even after 100 tests, the estimate of the success rate is very unreliable*

Hence, when a study presents a success rate, it should also provide an estimate of its standard deviation, but this is almost never the case. Therefore, in our example, for the effort of 70 evaluations and for 100 tests – which for its part can also only be roughly estimated – it is of the order of 17%.

Let us recall that in order to claim a success rate significantly different from another (at the probability threshold of 0.95), there must be a difference of at least $\frac{3}{number\ of\ tests}$ (Taillard *et al.* 2008).

Let us return to our first definition of an acceptable solution. It is too rigorous because it might be possible that a given execution never yields an acceptable solution, as far as we extend the effort, in which case, the difficulty would be infinite or, more precisely, overly large (see box below).

Let ε be the machine epsilon of our computer. In order to simplify, by overlooking "tricks" such as double-words, we shall say that this allows distinguishing $\frac{1}{\varepsilon}$ values in $[0, 1]$. Then, in the worst cases, if there are k acceptable solutions in $[0, 1]^D$, then a comprehensive search makes it possible to find one with an effort of $\frac{1}{\varepsilon^D} - k + 1$ evaluations. For ε, with a classic value of 10^{-16}, a tremendous effort is quickly reached when D increases.

In addition, it is usual that the optimizer be not designed to carry out an exhaustive search if necessary. At times, it loops endlessly over a finite set of positions; at other times, it completely randomly searches to the point of sampling several times the same position of the search space. For this second strategy, the probability that it finds an acceptable solution with effort E is

$$p = 1 - \left(1 - k\varepsilon^D\right)^E$$

Or, formulated otherwise, so that this probability be at least equal to a desirable value p_s, an effort has to be provided such as

$$E = \frac{\ln\left(1 - p_s\right)}{\ln\left(1 - k\varepsilon^D\right)}$$

For $k = 1$, $\varepsilon = 10^{-16}$, $D = 1$ and $p_s = 0.5$, this already gives us $E \simeq 6.2 \times 10^{15}$. For $D = 2$, software programs such as Matlab® output $E = Inf$.

Box 2.1. *When effort becomes excessive*

Therefore, our *desiderata* has to be somewhat relaxed. A simple way to do this is to give, at the same time as the tolerance threshold, a probability that is a desired success rate. The user's requirement then becomes something such as "For this problem, I want to get a solution at most equal to 0.001 and with a probability of at least 80%".

From such a requirement, it is possible to compare different optimizers and conclude which one is the most economical with regard to effort (see, for example, Chapter 6).

2.3. Difficulty vs complexity

When considering complexity theory, it is often thought that NP problems are more difficult than P problems. It should be remembered that P problems are those for which there is a resolution algorithm according to a given computational model, for example, a Turing machine, whose execution time (or, sometimes, the necessary memory space) increases in a polynomial fashion with the size of the problem. *Grosso modo*, for NP problems, the same definition can be re-used replacing "resolution" with "verification".

But this way of evaluating the difficulty of a problem presents at least three weak points:

– it is possible that in fact $P = NP$, since at the time of writing these lines (June 2018), neither this equality nor the strict inclusion $P \subset NP$ has been demonstrated;

– as seen in Chapter 1, the definition of the size is not univocal. A size can be defined, which exponentially increases with the number of dimensions of the search space, without noticing that there is another definition which increases in a polynomial manner only;

– above all, it is too binary to usefully classify problems by order of difficulty.

We could consider referring to complexity in Kolmogorov's sense, which would here be the size of the smallest algorithm able to generate the landscape under study. However, given that a very simple formula could create a very chaotic landscape, this would have nothing to do with the resolution difficulty that we are trying to estimate.

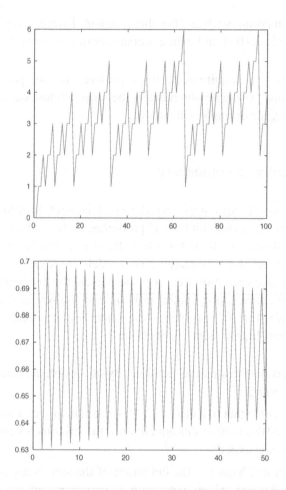

Figure 2.4. *Two functions of low Kolmogorov complexity, yet difficult for most optimizers. Their Matlab® codes are f=sum(de2bi([1:100]-1),2) and f(1)=0.7; for x=2:50 f(x)=3*f(x-1)*(1-f(x-1)); end*

2.4. Normalized roughness

If we expect to establish a gradation of difficulty levels, it would thus be better to focus on measures based on landscape analysis. For example, in (Weinberger 1990), the author considers *roughness* defined as the number of local optima. This is however very inadequate and even easily misleading, because it is possible to easily build two landscapes, the first one having more local minima than the second, but whose global minimum is yet easier for most optimizers to find (see Figure 2.5).

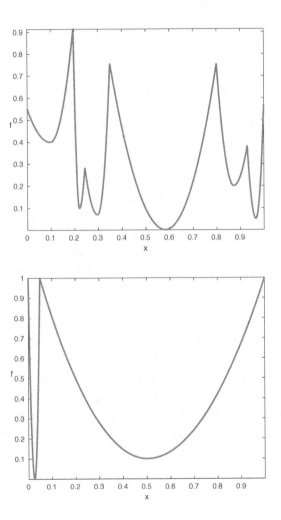

Figure 2.5. *Normalized roughness is not a good indicator of the difficulty. For the landscape at the top, it is equal to $\frac{5}{6} \simeq 0.83$, and only $\frac{1}{2} = 0.5$ for the one at the bottom, whose global minimum is yet more difficult to be found using a conventional optimizer*

For comparisons with other measures, I shall use here a normalized roughness defined by

$$\rho = \frac{number\ of\ local\ minima}{number\ of\ minima}$$

2.5. Measure $\delta_{r,\varepsilon}$

We have seen that roughness does not take into account the size of the basin of attraction of each minimum. Hence, in (Clerc 2005), I proposed as a difficulty measure the probability of not finding an acceptable solution "up to ε" (threshold of acceptability, possibly zero) by drawing a random point. Let us call it $\delta_{r,\varepsilon}$. Note that here ε is not machine epsilon, but a value given by the user, which must be larger.

Let $\mathbb{F}$ be the set of all functions (landscapes) of a definition space provided in a given space of values. It can be agreed that there is a "void" function $\oslash$ and that, with an obvious notation, $\delta_{r,\varepsilon}(\oslash) = 0$. Also, by definition, for any function f, we indeed have $\delta_{r,\varepsilon}(f) \geq 0$. Then, a tribe $\mathbb{A}$ can be defined (a σ-algebra) on $\mathbb{F}$ considering all of its subsets.

Here, $\mathbb{A}$ is finite (we are still within the context of a digital computer), and it is thus not possible to have the property of σ-additivity, and $\delta_{r,\varepsilon}$ is not a measure in the classical sense of the term. Nevertheless, it can be easily seen that this is a so-called "simply additive" measure, namely additive only for the union of a finite number of disjoint sets, which in practice is good enough because according to its definition itself, it is a probability (in the classic Kolmogorov's sense).

Box 2.2. *Is $\delta_{r,\varepsilon}$ really a measure?*

2.6. Measure δ_0

The measure $\delta_{r,\varepsilon}$ implicitly takes into account the size of the basins of attraction surrounding acceptable solutions, but not the size of those surrounding unacceptable local minima, whose existence yet contribute to increase the difficulty of the problem for a number of iterative optimizers which can become trapped for quite some time in these minima. It is thus also insufficient, just like roughness. It can be improved, and a measure δ_0 can be defined calculated by the algorithm 2.1, which takes into account not only the sizes of subdomains but also the relative values of minima. Section A.8 explains in detail the empirical reasons that justify this computational mode. This measure considers plateaus as flat basins. If it proved insufficient, it could still be improved at a measure δ_1, which would differentiate them from actual basins of attraction.

NOTE.– for simplicity, it is assumed here that there is only one global minimum. The definition domain is normalized at $[0, 1]^D$. The maximum value of the landscape is f_{max}.

(1) Decompose the domain of the landscape into m subdomains of sizes s_i

– s_{i^*} for the basin of attraction of the global minimum. Its minimum is equal to f_{i^*}.

– s_i, $i \neq i^*$ for the basins of attraction of local minima or plateaus, of values f_i.

(2) Combine and then transform the contributions to the difficulty of each domain (see section A.8)

$$\delta = \frac{1}{s_{i^*}} + \sum_{i \neq i^*} s_i \frac{f_{max} - f_{i^*}}{f_i - f_{i^*}} \qquad [2.1]$$

Since δ has values in $[1, \infty[$ it is useful to normalize it to facilitate graphical representations. Let $\delta_{uni} \in \ ]0, 1[$ be an arbitrary difficulty value for a unimodal landscape in dimension 1. The normalization on $[\delta_{min}, 1[$ can be done for example with

$$\delta_0 = 1 - \frac{1}{\sqrt{\delta} + \frac{\delta_{uni}}{1-\delta_{uni}}} \qquad [2.2]$$

3) (Unnecessary if only comparing same-size landscapes). Modify the difficulty according to the dimension of D. For more details see Chapter 6.

Algorithm 2.1. *Calculation of the difficulty δ_0 of a landscape.*

2.7. Measures non-NisB

Here, a *conjoint* measure or a *dependent* measure is a difficulty measure valid for an algorithm or, more generally, for a certain class of algorithms. The idea is not new; see, for example, Papadimitriou and Steiglitz (1978). Other useful references, such as Weise *et al.* (2009), are cited in the thesis by Weber (2013).

However, in these studies, the classes of algorithms under consideration are quite limited and, in addition, the problems are of the traveling salesman type. Nonetheless, we seek something more general, for both algorithms and problems.

Concerning algorithms, we are going to start from a characteristic shared by all "reasonable" iterative methods, that is, giving in practice satisfactory results with unbiased problems, which can be called the NisB strategy[1] (Clerc 2007).

The exploitation/exploration duality, sometimes called intensification/diversification, is well known and used by every iterative optimizer, according to varying strategies. Chapter 7 is specifically dedicated to this, because too often these concepts are used without being defined in a rigorous way.

The broad class of optimizers that we are interested in here is that of all those that at least give somewhat more importance to exploitation rather than to exploration. An exploitation strategy will be effective provided that, when approaching a "good" solution, there are more chances to find an even better one rather than when moving away. In short, "nearer is better" is true more often than vice versa. Note well that we are simply talking here about a probability greater than 0.5.

For example, the condition is always true for any unimodal landscape, and greedy algorithms, which are mainly

---

1 Nearer is Better (NisB). *Honi soit qui mal y pense!*

exploitation-based, are effective. However, obviously, for multimodal landscapes, they become easily stuck in local optima[2].

This notion of distance–value correlation can be formalized by making use of position triplets. Let N be the number of possible values (assumed to be the same for each dimension, to simplify). The definition space is I_N^D with $I_N = \left(0, \frac{1}{N-1}, \frac{1}{N-2}, \ldots, 1\right)$.

A *triplet* is a set $\{x_1, x_2, x_3\}$, $x_i \in I_N^D$, for which $x_1 \neq x_2$, $x_1 \neq x_3$ and $x_2 \neq x_3$. Let A_N be the set of all of triplets. For any function f of I_N^D in I_N, three subsets of triplets are defined[3]. To simplify the notation, it is assumed that every triplet is classified such that $f(x_1) \leq f(x_2) \leq f(x_3)$.

B-type triplets:

$$B_N := \begin{cases} f(x_2) < f(x_3) \\ |x_1 - x_2| < |x_1 - x_3| \end{cases}$$

W-type triplets:

$$W_N := \begin{cases} f(x_2) < f(x_3) \\ |x_1 - x_2| > |x_1 - x_3| \end{cases}$$

$L_N :=$ all others, so-called L-types. We have $L_N = L_{1,N} \cup L_{2,N}$, with $L_{1,N} := f(x_2) = f(x_3)$ and $L_{2,N} := |x_1 - x_2| = |x_1 - x_3|$.

For a given function, the *non-NisB difficulty* can then be defined as being the proportion of triplets of W- or L-type.

$$\delta_{\neg NisB} = \frac{|W_N| + |L_N|}{|A_N|} \qquad\qquad [2.3]$$

In practice, since the total number of triplets is very high, one will often proceed using random sampling to calculate an estimation of this measure (Monte Carlo method).

---

2 A few small examples can be found in Clerc (2015). See positive/negative correlation problems.

3 Their denominations B, W and L refer to the terms Better, Worse, Left.

REMARK 2.3.– One could assume that for a unimodal landscape, every triplet is of B-type. In fact, this is not the case; an example is given in section A.4.

Subsequently, we can say that the function is *reliable* if $\delta_{\neg NisB} < \frac{1}{2}$, *neutral* if $\delta_{\neg NisB} = \frac{1}{2}$ and *deceptive* if $\delta_{\neg NisB} > \frac{1}{2}$. A more detailed analysis is given in section 3.1.

2.7.1. *Deceptive vs disappointing*

It is also helpful to define what is a function of difficulty intermediary between reliable and deceptive. Consider the subset of triplets $A_N^* = \{x^*, x_2, x_3\}$, where x^* is a position of a global minimum and its partition in triplets of B-, W- and L-types, namely B_N^*, W_N^* and L_N^*, respectively. The related difficulty is given by

$$\delta_{\neg NisB}^* = \frac{|W_N^*| + |L_N^*|}{|A_N^*|}$$

The function will be known as *disappointing* if $\delta_{\neg NisB}^* > \frac{1}{2}$. The interest of this kind of functions is that when included in a set of tests, they allow a first quick discrimination between optimizers able to find their optimum almost as easily as for reliable functions and those for which they are already stumbling blocks.

A second level of discrimination will be given by deceptive functions: most optimizers struggle to find their minimum, some being even then not as good as random searching.

An example of each type of function is given in Figure 2.6.

2.7.2. *Measure consistency*

Since different difficulty measures are reasonably possible, it can be useful to verify that they are consistent with what experiments with several optimizers might give with various problems. In fact, this is not always the case, as we will see with two small test cases.

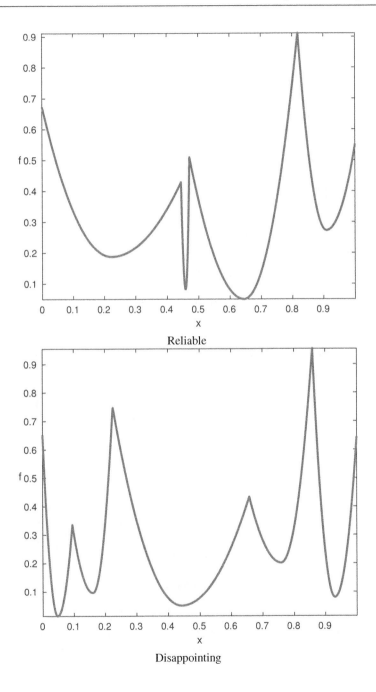

Reliable

Disappointing

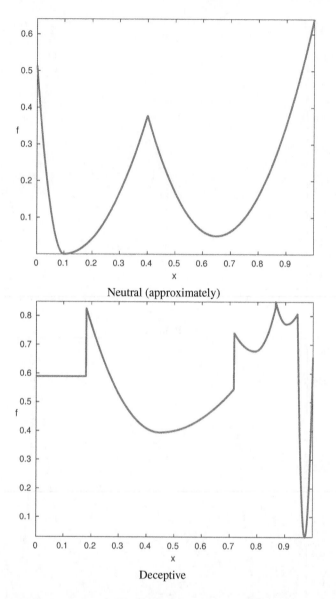

Neutral (approximately)

Deceptive

Figure 2.6. *Examples of four types of functions. A function is all the more deceptive if it comprises plateaus. Neutral functions are very rare. The one presented here is actually very slightly reliable (value 0.51)*

2.7.2.1. *First test case*

Table 2.1 presents a set of six landscapes and provides the success rates of three iterative stochastic optimizers of quite different principles: APS (Omran and Clerc 2017, APS), MVMO-SH (MVMO), GA-MPC (Elsayed *et al.* 2011) and SAMODE (Elsayed *et al.* 2011)[4]. The six landscapes under consideration have been built according to three criteria:

– in dimension 1, for readable representation. Naturally, tests have also been conducted in higher dimensions, but the point here is to illustrate the ideas presented;

– sometimes with plateaus;

– leading to a wide range of success rates for APS, to get sufficiently discriminating comparisons.

The success rates have been estimated over 10,000 executions. This number is much higher than that normally found in the literature, to ensure that rates are stabilized.

Figure 2.7 synthesizes a large amount of information and deserves detailed observations. The landscapes in abscissa are ordered by ascending order of difficulty δ_0, namely $(P_0, P_4, P_6, P_1, P_2, P_3, P_5)$. As a result, the corresponding curve is obviously increasing. This can be called the reference curve.

For the three optimizers, the curves represent the failure rates for a threshold of acceptability (tolerance threshold) of 0.0001 and a budget of evaluations.

With this threshold, the values of δ_r would be too small to be represented in the figure. However, our concern here is their ordering relation. The minimum of the local minima of the six landscapes is 0.2. Accordingly, for all the thresholds $\varepsilon < 0.2$, the measures $\delta_r(\varepsilon)$ will give the same ordering relation with the landscapes. Therefore, we can

---

4 In fact, versions significantly improved by myself, particularly for the last two.

take here $\varepsilon = 0.1$ just to obtain difficulty values of the same order of magnitude as failure rates.

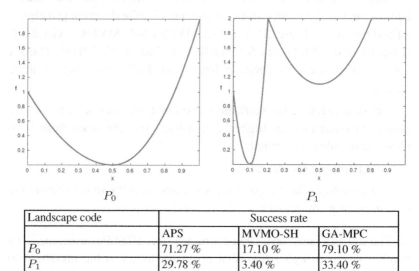

P_0 P_1

Landscape code	Success rate		
	APS	MVMO-SH	GA-MPC
P_0	71.27 %	17.10 %	79.10 %
P_1	29.78 %	3.40 %	33.40 %

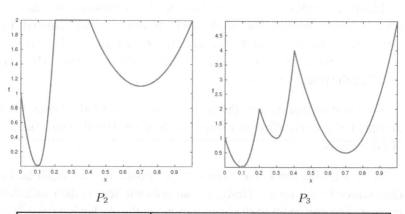

P_2 P_3

Landscape code	Success rate		
	APS	MVMO-SH	GA-MPC
P_2	27.50 %	4.50 %	32.75 %
P_3	26.50 %	3.40 %	28.85 %

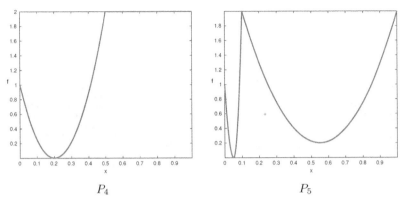

P_4 P_5

Landscape code	Success rate		
	APS	MVMO-SH	GA-MPC
P_4	54.50 %	9.10 %	66.45 %
P_5	12.49 %	1.50 %	7.25 %

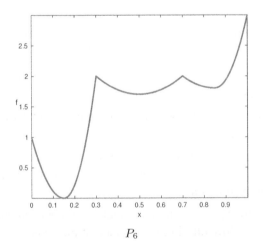

P_6

Landscape code	Success rate		
	APS	MVMO-SH	GA-MPC
P_6	40.80 %	5.30 %	49.85 %

Table 2.1. *Test case 1. Success rates of three stochastic iterative optimizers. Estimated over 10,000 tests of 50 evaluations, each for a threshold of acceptability of 0.0001*

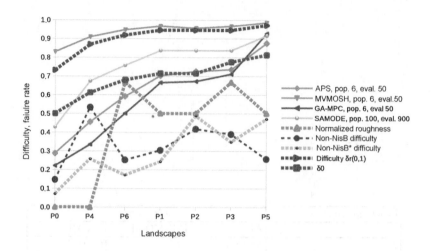

Figure 2.7. *With this test case, measures of difficulty δ_0, δ_r and even overall $\delta^*_{\neg NisB}$ properly recover the ordering relation of experimental failure rates, unlike the roughness and $\delta_{\neg NisB}$. These failure rates (for a threshold of acceptability of 0.0001) are estimated over 10,000 executions. For a color version of this image, see www.iste.co.uk/clerc/iterative.zip*

The findings:

– the curve of δ_r is increasing. This indicates that this measure is consistent with δ_0;

– the normalized roughness and the measure $\delta_{\neg NisB}$ are not good indicators. This is quite logical because they do not use the knowledge of the minimum sought after;

– the measure $\delta^*_{\neg NisB}$ is already much better, but sometimes tends to overestimate the difficulty in the presence of plateaus;

– the curves of failure rates are increasing. Therefore, the theoretical difficulty δ_0 achieves a good prediction of the performance of algorithms under consideration. This is particularly interesting because it is based only on the sizes of the domains and the values of minima. Therefore, it will be possible to easily build landscapes of given δ_0

measures. It should be noted that it is still in terms of ordering relation on landscapes.

It is not the purpose of this study, but in actual values, it can be seen in Figure 2.7 that APS and GA-MPC have similar efficiencies (in fact, with a more comprehensive set of more difficult problems, APS is significantly better (Omran and Clerc 2017, Omran and Clerc 2016)) and that SAMODE is clearly much worse, all the more given that its Matlab® code does not work for populations smaller than 80 and that in order to enable it to perform roughly as many iterations as the others, it was necessary to provide it with a higher budget (900 vs 50). Nonetheless, see Chapter 6 for problems for which SAMODE is instead much more efficient.

Concerning MVMO-SH, its low success rates classify it as being very mediocre.

Box 2.3. *Test case 1. Comparisons of efficiency*

2.7.2.2. *Second test case*

Actually, the first test case is biased in favor of δ_r. In fact, in this case, the sole criterion which intervenes in its calculation is the size of the basin of attraction of the global minimum, which correctly yields $(P_0, P_4, P_6, P_1, P_2, P_3, P_5)$ defined by δ_0. Does this mean that other structural elements have no influence? To answer this question, we use a second set of tests, derived from the first one, but in which all global basins now have the same size.

By construction, therefore, the measure δ_r will give us the same value for landscapes, while, as indicated in Table 2.2 and Figure 2.8, this is not the case for the optimizers that have been tested. Consequently, unlike what the first test case might suggest, it is not reliable as an indicator of difficulty perceived by these optimizers.

Since the measure $\delta_{\neg NisB}$ is already not working well with test case 1, we are still left with measures δ_0 and $\delta^*_{\neg NisB}$. According to

Figure 2.8, the latter is also not consistent with the three optimizers tested, unless only landscapes with no plateaus are considered (Figure 2.9).

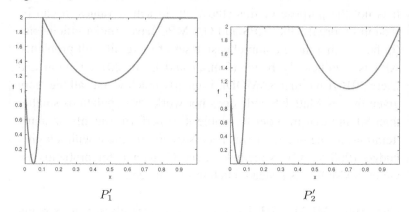

Landscape code	Success rate		
	APS	MVMO-SH	GA-MPC
P_1'	18.87%	1.54%	14.34%
P_2'	17.07%	1.70%	13.74%

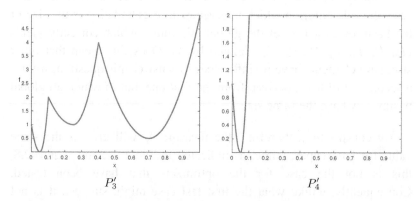

Landscape code	Success rate		
	APS	MVMO-SH	GA-MPC
P_3'	16.79%	1.74%	12.34%
P_4'	58.15%	1.90%	18.10%

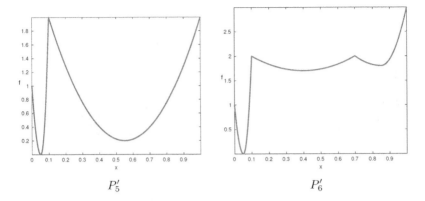

$$P_5'$$ $$P_6'$$

Landscape code	Success rate		
	APS	MVMO-SH	GA-MPC
P_5'	12.49%	1.72%	7.56%
P_6'	19.83%	1.66%	17.74%

Table 2.2. *Test case 2. Success rates of three stochastic iterative optimizers. Estimated over 10,000 tests of 50 evaluations each for a threshold of acceptability of 0.0001. The landscapes are derived from those of test case 1 by standardizing the size of the global basin to 0.1*

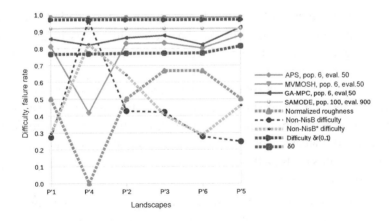

Figure 2.8. *Consistencies (test case 2). Only the measure δ_0 shows good consistency. For a color version of this image, see www.iste.co.uk/clerc/iterative.zip*

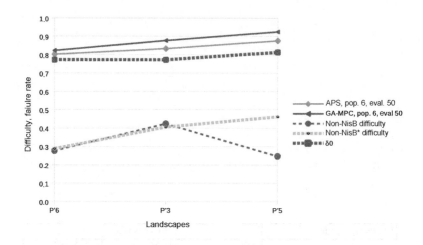

Figure 2.9. *Consistencies without plateaus (test case 2). In this case, if it is not possible to use δ_0, due to lack of information on the structure of the landscape; $\delta^*_{\neg NisB}$ is acceptable. For a color version of this image, see www.iste.co.uk/clerc/iterative.zip*

Thus, to summarize, in the presence of a set of landscapes, in other words a test case:

– if the structure of each landscape (basins, plateaus) is known, its difficulty can be assessed by δ_0 and the resulting classification will have a good chance of being the one that will be found by applying a good iterative optimizer. In practice, this can only be done if the landscapes have been explicitly built precisely from basins and plateaus with defined characteristics (see Chapter 4). In classic test cases, only the global minimum is known in general. It is then necessary to detect basins and plateaus. This may require considerable computation time. Moreover, this is also a flaw common to all methods based on landscape analysis made *a posteriori*;

– if the structure is not known, then $\delta^*_{\neg NisB}$ can be used, provided that landscapes do not comprise significant plateaus. This is the case of the classic test cases studied in Chapter 5.

MVMO-SH and SAMODE confirm that they have high failure rates (Figure 2.8). A remarkable point is that these rates are almost constant. It can be deduced that the main criterion that determines the effectiveness of these optimizers is the size of the global basin. Without even studying their source codes, this strongly suggests that they perform too much random sampling and make bad use of the information on the landscape collected during the research process.

Here APS is better than GA-MPC, especially on the landscape P'_4, which comprises a broad plateau. This is due to its stagnation detection mechanism, which for its part wisely indicates when it is necessary to increase the number of random explorations, as an effective way to escape a plateau, and when, on the contrary, it is rather necessary to perform exploitation, which is an efficient way to find the low point of a basin.

Box 2.4. *Test case 2. Comparison of efficiencies*

2.7.2.3. *Discussion*

It could be sustained that measures directly based on the structure of the landscape are intrinsic and thus valid for all possible algorithms. However, in reality, as already mentioned, the same problem may prove to be difficult for a given algorithm and easier for another. For example, on the landscape of Figure 2.10, the success rate of the greedy algorithm (purely greedy as its name suggests see section A.11) for the acceptability threshold of 0.0001 is only 0.07%, whereas it is 100% for APS, for the same population of six individuals and the same budget of 2,400 evaluations.

We thus repeat that these measures have no absolute value and only allow classifying problems for a given algorithm or, more precisely, for a class of algorithms, namely those that implicitly or explicitly assume that "nearer is better", at least in probability.

The measure δ_r is simple to estimate with a given landscape, since a very large number of points have to be sampled and the proportion of those whose value is less than the acceptability threshold have to be calculated. Despite the fact that computation time can be considerable, the procedure is much easier to achieve than detecting basins, plateaus and local minima. It can thus be used to classify problems of test cases existing in the literature. Nevertheless, it requires the definition of an arbitrary threshold of acceptability. In addition, this classification is not very discriminating, because it assigns the same rank to landscapes that have the same size of global basin, regardless of other structural features.

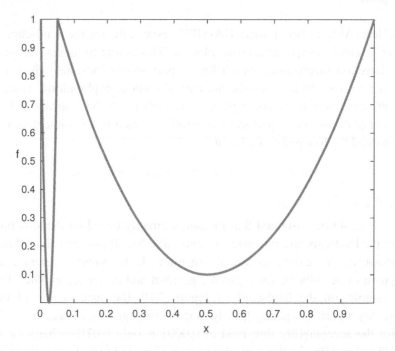

Figure 2.10. *An easy problem for APS but difficult for greedy*

The measure $\delta^*_{\neg NisB}$ is almost also easy to estimate, by means of sampling a very large number of triplets, provided that the position of the global minimum is known, or if not, that of the best solution found so far. It does not require an acceptability threshold to be *a priori* defined. In this sense, it is more general than δ_r and thereby should be preferred to it (see Chapter 5).

2.8. Perceived difficulty

Referring to APS, MVMO-SH, GA-MPC or others as optimizers is somewhat a misnomer. In reality, an optimizer is a composite object, comprising an algorithm and parameters. Therefore, all other parameters being the same, APS with a population of six individuals, which may be denoted by APS(6), is not the same optimizer as APS(90). Since the difficulty of a problem, in accordance with definition 2.1, involves the effort to be provided, it can therefore be expected that it is different for these two optimizers. It can be called perceived difficulty (implied: by the optimizer).

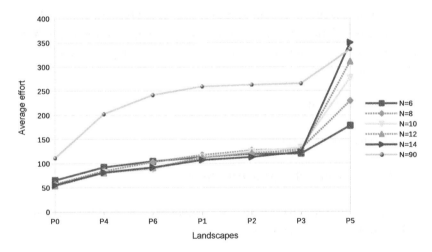

Figure 2.11. *Practical difficulty for APS of the test case* $(P_0, \ldots, P_6)$ *according to the size* N *of the population used. Threshold acceptability: 0.0001; desired success rate: 80%. The value* $N = 90$ *is automatically calculated by standard APS for dimension 1. For a color version of this image, see www.iste.co.uk/clerc/iterative.zip*

With our small test set 1, Figure 2.11 presents for APS the changes in the estimated perceived difficulties (that is, of average efforts, as the number of evaluations) as a function of the size N of the population for a threshold of acceptability of 0.0001 and a likelihood of success equal to at least 80%.

The fact that all the curves are increasing confirms a good agreement of these estimates with the theoretical difficulty δ_0 and, at the same time, with the classification given by the estimation of failure rates. This is an interesting point, because these failure rates can be easier to estimate than perceived difficulties. In fact, for these latter, it is necessary to try different increasing values of the effort (the number of evaluations), until the desired success probability is obtained (see the pseudo-code in Box 2.5).

Naturally, with such simple problems, APS(90) – that is, with the standard population in the first dimension – is not as good as others, because just the random initialization itself already "consumes" 90 evaluations.

N = population size

τ = desired success rate

$nbExp$ = number of experiments (tests)

FE_{min} = minimum number of evaluations of positions in the definition space of the problem

S_{min} = minimum number of successful sequences before evaluating the average effort

σ = coefficient of accuracy on the estimation of the average effort

To build Figure 2.11, and for each value of N, the parameters are $\tau = 0.8$, $nbExp = 100$, $FE_{min} = 60$, $S_{min} = 20$ and $\sigma = 0.1$.

Pseudo-code
s=0; effort=FE_{min}; effStd=FE_{min};

While effStd>σ×effort % Loop s, to ensure

% a convergence of the average effort
sr=0;
FEmax=FE_{min}
While sr<τ % Loop sr. We will increase FEmax

% as long as necessary
ok=0;

For n=1:$nbExp$ % Loop n, to estimate
% the success rate
fmin(n)=XXX(N,problem,FEmax);
If fmin≤ τ ok=ok+1;

sr=ok/$nbExp$; % Estimated success rate
FEmax=FEmax+1;

% Here the loop sr is complete and, therefore,
% the success rate is acceptable
s=s+1;

sequence(s)=FEmax; % The value of the effort is stored
If s≥ S_{min}

effort=Average(sequence);
effstd=deviation_type(sequence);

% Here the loop is complete
Print effort and effStd

Box 2.5. *Estimation of the perceived difficulty for the optimizer XXX*

3

Landscape Typology

In dimension $D = 1$, on a digital computer, it can be considered that the definition space contains N equidistant values, namely $I_N = \left\{0, \frac{1}{N-1}, \frac{2}{N-1}, \cdots, 1\right\}$, similarly to the space of values. A landscape is then a mapping from I_N onto I_N, more generally, in dimension D, from I_N^D onto I_N. In general, we have $N = 2^{K-1} + 1$, where K is an integer such as 32, 64, 128 and so on.

To establish a typology of the set of landscapes, I shall consider only the following three criteria, relatively easy to take into account in practice:

– the distance–value correlation;

– plateaus (their size, their value);

– minima (basins of attraction and values).

A priori, the relative positions of basins of attraction could play a role, but experimentally, it proves to be of little significance (see section A.8). In this quite formal chapter, we shall talk about functions rather than landscapes, and triplets will be largely used. Remember a few definitions, seen in section 2.7:

A *triplet* is a set $\{x_1, x_2, x_3\}$, $x_i \in I_N^D$, for which $x_1 \neq x_2$, $x_1 \neq x_3$ and $x_2 \neq x_3$.

For every function f from I_N^D onto I_N, three subsets of triplets are defined (to simplify the notation, it is assumed that any triplet is classified such that $f(x_1) \leq f(x_2) \leq f(x_3)$):

B-type triplets, for which "nearer is better"

$$B_N := \begin{cases} f(x_2) < f(x_3) \\ |x_1 - x_2| < |x_1 - x_3| \end{cases}$$

W-type triplets, for which "nearer is worse"

$$W_N := \begin{cases} f(x_2) < f(x_3) \\ |x_1 - x_2| > |x_1 - x_3| \end{cases}$$

$L_N :=$ all others, so-called L-types.

Finally, the non-NisB degree of difficulty is given by:

$$\delta_{\neg NisB} = \frac{|W_N| + |L_N|}{|A_N|}$$

3.1. Reliable functions, misleading and neutral

Let us define a partition of the set $\mathbb{F}$ of all the functions:

– $\mathbb{F}_b$, for which $\mu(W) < \mu(B)$. These functions are here called *reliable*;

– $\mathbb{F}_w$, for which $\mu(W) > \mu(B)$ and called *deceptive*;

– $\mathbb{F}_n = \mathbb{F} - \mathbb{F}_b - \mathbb{F}_w$, known as *neutral*.

On $\mathbb{F}$, a measure of the subset $\mathbb{Y}$ is defined as

$$\nu(\mathbb{Y}) = \limsup_{N \to \infty} \frac{[\![\mathbb{Y} \cap \mathbb{F}_N]\!]}{[\![\mathbb{F}]\!]}$$

3.1.1. *Dimension* $D = 1$

In dimension 1, we have $\llbracket \mathbb{F} \rrbracket = N^N$. We are trying to estimate the proportion of each function type (reliable, deceptive and neutral). Recall that by definition, in a triplet (x_1, x_2, x_3), every element is different. To simplify the notation, the ranks of values in I_N are considered rather than these values themselves. For example, the triplet $\left(0, \frac{1}{N-1}, \frac{1}{N-2}\right)$ will be coded $(1, 2, 3)$. In fact, for this analysis, $\{1, 2, \cdots, N\}$ can also be considered instead of I_N.

There are three different cases:

1) the triplet is $(n, n + k, n + 2k)$. We can symbolically denote $x_1 \frown x_2 \frown x_3$, meaning that $x_2 - x_1 = x_3 - x_2$;

2) the triplet is $(n, n + k, n + k + k')$ with $k' < k$. Symbolically, $x_1 \frown\frown x_2 \frown x_3$, that is, $x_2 - x_1 > x_3 - x_2$;

3) the triplet is $(n, n + k, n + k + k')$ with $k' > k$. Symbolically, $x_1 \frown x_2 \frown\frown x_3$.

Experimentally (for example, see Table 3.1), it seems that, considering all the functions, they define as many B-type triplets as they do W-type triplets, namely

$$\sum_{n=1}^{N^N} \llbracket B_{N,\mathbb{F}(n)} \rrbracket = \sum_{n=1}^{N^N} \llbracket W_{N,\mathbb{F}(n)} \rrbracket \qquad [3.1]$$

where $B_{N,\mathbb{F}(n)}$ (resp. $W_{N,\mathbb{F}(n)}$) is the set of triplets of type B (resp. W) for the function $\mathbb{F}(n)$ from I_N onto I_N. It is however necessary to demonstrate it. To this end, one also defines $L_{N,\mathbb{F}(n)}$ as the set of triplets that, for the function $\mathbb{F}(n)$, are neither in $B_{N,\mathbb{F}(n)}$ nor in $W_{N,\mathbb{F}(n)}$.

Finding the exact formulas by enumeration is not inherently difficult, but quite tedious. Table 3.2 summarizes the results. It is here assumed that N is odd, but similar formulas could be found for even N. For the last three columns, the last line gives the sum of the three values above, weighted by the number of triplets of each case (the first column).

Triplet			$\sum_{n=1}^{N^N} [\![B_{N,\mathbb{F}(n)}]\!]$	$\sum_{n=1}^{N^N} [\![W_{N,\mathbb{F}(n)}]\!]$	$\sum_{n=1}^{N^N} [\![L_{N,\mathbb{F}(n)}]\!]$
3	4	5	750	750	1,625
2	4	5	1,250	1,000	875
2	3	5	1,000	1,250	875
2	3	4	750	750	1,625
1	4	5	1,250	1,000	875
1	3	5	750	750	1,625
1	3	4	1,250	1,000	875
1	2	5	1,000	1,250	875
1	2	4	1,000	1,250	875
1	2	3	750	750	1,625
		Total	9,750	9,750	11,750

Table 3.1. $N = 5$. *The triplets are here the ranks of the values (1 for 0, 2 for $\frac{1}{N-1}$, etc.). For every triplet, we count how many times it is of type* B *(resp.* W *or* L*) for the set of the* N^N *functions*

Let us look at the ratios $\sigma_B = \frac{s_B}{s_B+s_W+s_L}$, $\sigma_W = \frac{s_W}{s_B+s_W+s_L}$ and $\sigma_L = \frac{s_L}{s_B+s_W+s_L}$.

On a computer with a very small machine-epsilon, N becomes very large and then tends towards a limit, as described in Table 3.1.

From this table, one can immediately draw interesting conclusions. For example, as for L-type triplets the ratio $\frac{\sum_{n=1}^{N^N} [\![L_{N,\mathbb{F}(n)}]\!]}{[\![A_N]\!][\![\mathbb{F}_N]\!]}$ is equal to $\frac{8N^3-19N^2+8N-1}{4N^3(N-2)}$, it tends to zero as $\frac{2}{N}$ when N tends to infinity. This means that on I (the limit of I_N) the set $\mathbb{F}_l$ of neutral functions is negligible.

Now consider the proportions of reliable functions (namely for which $\mu(B) > \mu(W)$), deceptive and neutral, respectively ϱ_B, ϱ_W and ϱ_L. The exact formulas depending on N are not (for the moment) known, but we can nonetheless get an idea of their behavior when $N \to \infty$.

Case	Number of triplets	$\sum_{n=1}^{N^N}\left[\!\left[B_{N,\mathbb{F}(n)}\right]\!\right]$	$\sum_{n=1}^{N^N}\left[\!\left[W_{N,\mathbb{F}(n)}\right]\!\right]$	$\sum_{n=1}^{N^N}\left[\!\left[L_{N,\mathbb{F}(n)}\right]\!\right]$
$x_1 \frown x_2 \frown x_3$	$\dfrac{(N-1)^2}{4}$	$\dfrac{N^{N-2}\left(2N^2-3N+1\right)}{6}$	$\dfrac{N^{N-2}\left(2N^2-3N+1\right)}{6}$	$\dfrac{N^{N-2}\left(N^2+3N+1\right)}{6}$
$x_1 \frown (\frown x_2 \frown x_3)$	$\dfrac{N(N-1)(N-2)}{12} - \dfrac{(N-1)^2}{8}$	$\dfrac{N^{N-1}(N-1)}{2}$	$\dfrac{N^{N-2}(N-1)^2}{2}$	$\dfrac{N^{N-2}(3N-1)}{2}$
$x_1 \frown (x_2 \frown (x_3$	$\dfrac{N(N-1)(N-2)}{12} - \dfrac{(N-1)^2}{8}$	$\dfrac{N^{N-2}(N-1)^2}{2}$	$\dfrac{N^{N-1}(N-1)}{2}$	$\dfrac{N^{N-2}(3N-1)}{2}$
Sum (weighted)	$\dfrac{N(N-1)(N-2)}{6}$	$s_B = \dfrac{N^{N-2}(N-1)^2\left(4N^3-12N^2+7N-1\right)}{48}$	$s_W = \dfrac{N^{N-2}(N-1)^2\left(4N^3-12N^2+7N-1\right)}{48}$	$s_L = \dfrac{N^{N-2}\left(8N^4-27N^3+27N^2-9N+1\right)}{24}$

Table 3.2. *Summary of the numbers of triplets*

	N	Evolution for $N \to \infty$
$\dfrac{\text{number of } x_1\frown x_2\frown x_3}{2\times \text{number of } x_1\frown\frown x_2\frown x_3}$	$3\dfrac{N-1}{2N^2-7N+3}$	↘ 0
σ_B	$\dfrac{(N-1)^2\left(2N^2-5N-1\right)}{4N^3(N-2)}$	↗ $\frac{1}{2}$
σ_W	$\dfrac{(N-1)^2(2N-1)}{4N^3}$	↗ $\frac{1}{2}$
σ_L	$1-\varrho_B-\varrho_w$	↘ 0
$\dfrac{\sigma_B}{\sigma_W}$	$\dfrac{2N^2-5N-1}{(2N-1)(N-2)}$	↗ 1

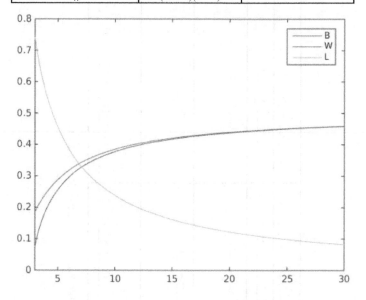

Figure 3.1. *A few ratios and their limits. Neutral triplets (of type* L*) become negligible compared to others. Moreover, σ_B is always smaller than σ_W, but the difference tends to zero. For a color version of this image, see www.iste.co.uk/clerc/iterative.zip*

According to Figure 3.1, we have $\underset{\to}{\sigma_L} = \lim_{N\to\infty}\sigma_L = 0$ and $\underset{\to}{\sigma_B} = \underset{\to}{\sigma_W} = \frac{1}{2}$ and the linear system

$$
\begin{cases}
\underset{\to}{\sigma_B} = a\underset{\to}{\varrho_B} + (1-a)\underset{\to}{\varrho_W}\\
\underset{\to}{\sigma_W} = (1-d)\,\underset{\to}{\varrho_B} + d\underset{\to}{\varrho_W}
\end{cases}
$$

with $1 \geq a > \frac{1}{2}$ and $1 \geq d > \frac{1}{2}$. This implies

$$
\begin{cases}
\underset{\rightarrow}{\varrho_B} = \frac{1}{a+d-1}\left(d\underset{\rightarrow}{\sigma_B} + (a-1)\,\underset{\rightarrow}{\sigma_W} \right) \\[2mm]
\underset{\rightarrow}{\varrho_W} = \frac{1}{a+d-1}\left((d-1)\,\underset{\rightarrow}{\sigma_B} + a\underset{\rightarrow}{\sigma_W} \right)
\end{cases}
$$

and thus

$$
\underset{\rightarrow}{\varrho_W} - \underset{\rightarrow}{\varrho_B} = \frac{1}{a+d-1}\left(\underset{\rightarrow}{\sigma_W} - \underset{\rightarrow}{\sigma_B} \right) = 0,
$$

which leads to the following theorem.

THEOREM 3.1.– *Half of the functions of I in I are deceptive and half are reliable.*

3.1.1.1. *Dimension $D \geq 2$*

Here, again, there is no known formula. However, it is possible to experiment using the Monte Carlo method. For a given dimension, a large number of functions are randomly generated; then, one counts how many are of each type. The process is very simple, but obviously takes rather a long computation time. The results suggest the generalization of Theorem 3.1.

CONJECTURE 3.1.– *For any dimension D, half of the functions of I^D in I are deceptive and half are reliable.*

As we have seen, the conjecture is true in dimension one. For higher dimensions, in addition to experimental results, we may also resort to "ergodic"-type reasoning:

– any triplet can be rearranged such as to have $\|x_1 - x_2\| \leq \|x_1 - x_3\|$;

– the triplets for which there is equality can be ignored, that is, $\|x_1 - x_2\| = \|x_1 - x_3\|$;

– if we randomly draw the values $f(x_1)$, $f(x_2)$ and $f(x_3)$ and consider all possible cases (such as for example, $(f(x_1) > f(x_2)) \wedge (f(x_2) < f(x_3)) \wedge (f(x_3) < f(x_1))$), it is then found that the probability that the triplet be of B-type is equal to $\frac{1}{2}$.

3.2. Plateaus

In the analysis of relations between the presence, or absence, of plateaus and the nature of the function (reliable, deceptive), it is possible to find formulas in both dimension 1 as higher dimensions, but they are slightly different.

3.2.1. *Dimension* $D = 1$

THEOREM 3.2.– *A function without plateau can be deceptive.*

To find it, it should be enough to show one example at least. We shall give several of them. When the number of points of the definition space is low (remember that it is always finite with a digital computer), finding a deceptive function without plateaus is easy (see Figure 3.2).

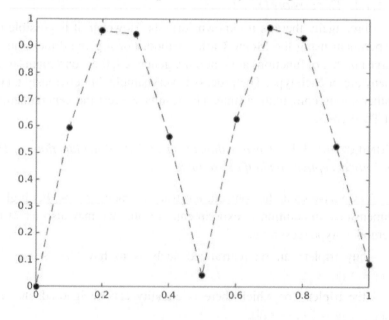

Figure 3.2. *A function defined on 11 points.*
Degree of non-NisB difficulty $= 0.58$

Even a simple function can be deceptive (see Figure 3.3).

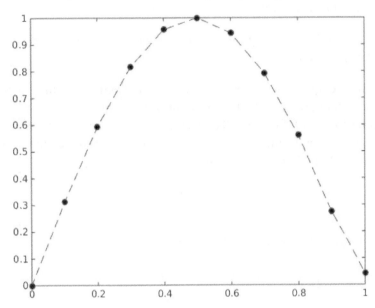

Figure 3.3. *A simple function defined on 11 points. Degree of difficulty 0.57*

This may seem counterintuitive, but we shall not forget that with N points, only $\frac{N(N-1)(N-2)}{6}$ triplets can be defined. Therefore, for $N = 11$, the number of triplets is 165, and hence, it is easy to have $\mu(B) < \mu(W)$.

Note that a small value of N is common when the "positions" are binary strings. It is then very simple to build functions that are difficult for conventional optimizers (Goldberg 1992).

An example is given in section A.4. Nevertheless, experiments suggest the following conjecture:

CONJECTURE 3.2.– *For a given dimension, the degree of difficulty of a Lipschitz function without plateaus is upper bounded by a constant strictly smaller than 1.*

In fact, it seems that this upper bound is an increasing function of the Lipschitz constant[1].

THEOREM 3.3.– *Half of the functions without plateaus are deceptive and half are reliable.*

Another question is "how many deceptive functions are there among those without plateaus?". Let us count. It is possible to find a formula similar to that of Table 3.2. The factor N^N should simply be replaced by another; for example, the number of functions for which the triplets of ranks $(1, 2, 3)$ are of type B becomes

$$(N - 1)^{N-3} \frac{N\left(N^2 - 3N + 2\right)}{3}$$

and, for the triplets such as $(1, 3, 5)$, we have

$$(N - 2)^2 (N - 1)^{N-5} \frac{N\left(N^2 - 3N + 2\right)}{3}$$

However, more kinds of triplets must be taken into account, but the important point is that, again, s_B and s_W are polynomials in N of degree N^3 (and with the same first coefficient), whereas for s_L, the degree is only N^2. Thereby (even if it seems a little strange), we still have σ_B and σ_W tending to $\frac{1}{2}$ when N increases, and even with $\sigma_B < \sigma_W$. The only difference is that the increase rate is lower than when all functions are considered (that is, with or without plateau).

Therefore, finally, even functions without plateaus are not particularly reliable.

THEOREM 3.4.– *Most functions have at least one plateau.*

In the finite case, both the definition space $(x_1, x_2, \ldots, x_N)$ and the space of values have N points. A minimal two-point plateau (2-plateau for short) is defined in x_k by $([x_k, x_{k+1}], f(x_k))$ if $f(x_{k+1}) = f(x_k)$.

---

1 Moreover, given that on a digital computer all functions are Lipschitzian, this suggests here opportunities for improving deterministic optimizers.

Having at least one plateau is equivalent to having at least a 2-plateau. Let us study this case.

The probability p that $f(x_{k+1}) = f(x_k)$ is $p = \frac{N}{N^2} = \frac{1}{N}$. Thus, the probability of not having 2-plateau independently of $k \in \{1, 2, \ldots, N-1\}$ is $\left(1 - \frac{1}{N}\right)^{N-1}$. Finally, the probability of having at least a 2-plateau is

$$S_N = 1 - \left(1 - \frac{1}{N}\right)^{N-1} \qquad [3.2]$$

In other words, the number of functions without plateaus is $N(N-1)^{N-1}$. For $N = 2$, the probability S_N is obviously 0.5, then it increases quickly towards a limit, as can be seen in Figure 3.5.

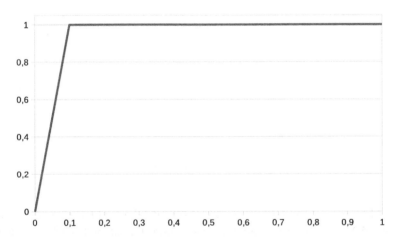

Figure 3.4. *Needle function for $a = 0.1$*

To find this limit, we can take the logarithm

$$\begin{cases} \ln(1 - S_N) = (N-1)\ln\left(1 - \frac{1}{N}\right) \\ \sim -(N-1)\frac{1}{N} \\ \sim -1 + \frac{1}{N} \end{cases}$$

which gives

$$\nu\left(\mathbb{F}_p\right) = \lim_{N\to\infty} S_N = 1 - e^{-1} \simeq 0.632 \qquad [3.3]$$

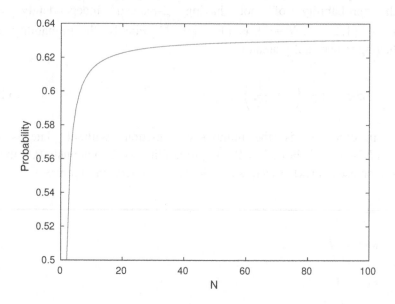

Figure 3.5. *In dimension one, probability of having at least a 2-plateau based on N, common size of the definition space and of the space of values*

Therefore, about 63% of the functions of $\mathbb{F}$ have at least one plateau. Since 50% functions are reliable, this implies that at the least 13% of the functions are both reliable and with plateau. Or, formulated otherwise, at least 26% of the functions with one plateau at least are reliable.

This is obviously due to the fact that the proportion of plateaus can be small and, in this case, the function is not deceptive. Hence, the following conjecture can be proposed:

CONJECTURE 3.3.– *If the proportion of plateau(s) is greater than a certain value, depending on dimension, then the function may not be reliable.*

For example, consider the Needle N function defined on $[0, 1]$ as

$$f(x) = \frac{x}{a} \text{ if } x \le a$$
$$1 \text{ otherwise}$$

A triplet is then of type B if at least two of its elements are smaller than a. The probability of this case is $3a^2 - 2a^3$. Therefore, the function is deceptive as soon as this probability is lower than $\frac{1}{2}$, or more precisely as soon as the size $1 - a$ of the plateau is larger than $\frac{1}{2}$.

REMARK 3.1.– The likelihood of having an m-plateau for a given N is

$$S_{N,m} = 1 - \left(1 - \frac{1}{N^{m-1}}\right)^{N-m+1}$$

It is a decreasing function of m, but when N increases, the limit is the same for all m.

Let us call *plateau ratio*, the measure of the set of points belonging to a plateau[2]. Then, a more general question is "What is the proportion of functions for which the plateau ratio is at least equal to α?". By applying the same method as above, it can easily be found that the limit value when $N \to \infty$ is

$$\nu(\mathbb{F}_{p,\alpha}) = P_\alpha = 1 - e^{-(1-\alpha)}$$

Moreover, as shown in Figure 3.6 and as intuitively expected, this value is a decreasing function of α. At the extreme, for $\alpha = 100\%$, there are only N possible functions, fully "flat". Compared to the set of all the functions, of size N^N, their proportion limit is indeed zero.

3.2.2. Dimension $D \ge 2$

For dimensions greater than one, the formula [3.2] becomes slightly different. The probability p of having a minimal plateau (which is a $D+1$-vertex polyhedron) at a given "position" is now $\frac{1}{N^D}$.

---

2 Recall that we are working on $[0, 1]$, and hence, it can actually be referred to as a ratio.

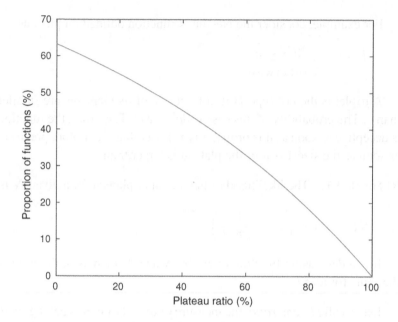

Figure 3.6. *Proportion of functions vs plateau ratio. The larger the total size of the plateau, the fewer possible functions there are*

The number of such polyhedra is $2^D (N-1)^D$ and the likelihood of having at least one plateau is

$$S_{N,D} = 1 - \left(1 - \frac{1}{N^D}\right)^{2^D(N-1)^D}$$

where

$$\nu(F_{p,D}) = \lim_{N \to \infty} S_{N,D} = 1 - e^{-2^D}$$

REMARK 3.2.– This formula is not valid for $D = 1$, and this probability quickly increases with D. For example, $\nu(\mathbb{F}_{p,3}) \simeq 0.9997$. In practice, as soon as D is slightly large, every function has at least one minimal plateau.

3.3. Multimodal functions

To facilitate the analysis, four cases can be distinguished:
– only one global minimum and dimension 1;
– only one global minimum and dimension higher than 1;
– several global minima and dimension 1;
– several global minima and dimension higher than 1.

3.3.1. *Functions with single global minimum*

3.3.1.1. *Dimension $D = 1$*

Let $\mathbb{F}_{g,N}$ be the set of functions of $\mathbb{F}_N$ with only one single global minimum. They may nonetheless have several local minima. Their number is given by

$$\llbracket \mathbb{F}_{g,N} \rrbracket = N \sum_{k=1}^{N-1} (N-k)^{N-1} = \mathfrak{B}_N(N) - \mathfrak{B}_N(0)$$

by applying a variant of the Faulhaber formula Conway and Guy (1996) and where $\mathfrak{B}_N(m)$ is the Bernoulli polynomial of degree N evaluated at m. In fact, there are N positions for a global minimum of rank (value) k. This rank is in $\{1, 2, \cdots, N-1\}$, and the $N-1$ other ranks of the function are in $\{k+1, \cdots, N\}$, that is, they have $N-k$ possible values.

Therefore, the measure of $\mathbb{F}_g$ is thus[3]

$$\begin{aligned}
\nu(\mathbb{F}_g) &= \limsup_{N\to\infty} \frac{\llbracket \mathbb{F}_{g,N} \cap F_g \rrbracket}{N^N} \\
&= \lim_{N\to\infty} \frac{\mathfrak{B}_N(N)}{N^N} \qquad\qquad\qquad [3.4]\\
&= \frac{1}{e-1} \simeq 0.582
\end{aligned}$$

---

3 Synopsis of the demonstration. We have the classic formula $\mathfrak{B}_N(N) = \sum_{k=0}^{N} \binom{N}{k} \mathfrak{B}_k N^{N-k}$ and the generating function of the Bernoulli numbers $\mathfrak{B}_k$ yields $\frac{1}{e-1} = \sum_{k=0}^{\infty} \frac{\mathfrak{B}_k}{k!}$. Then, $\frac{\mathfrak{B}_N(N)}{N^N} = \sum_{k=0}^{N} \frac{N!}{(N-k)!N^k} \frac{\mathfrak{B}_k}{k!}$, and one should bear in mind that $\lim_{N\to\infty} \frac{N!}{(N-k)!N^k} = 1$.

3.3.1.2. *Dimension $D \geq 2$*

We have $[\![\mathbb{F}_N]\!] = N^{N^D}$ and

$$[\![\mathbb{F}_{g,N}]\!] = N^D \sum_{k=1}^{N-1} (N-k)^{N^D-1} = \mathfrak{B}_{N^D}(N) - \mathfrak{B}_{N^D}(0)$$

from which, if $D > 1$

$$\nu\left(\mathbb{F}_{\mathrm{g},D}\right) = \lim_{N \to \infty} \sum_{k=0}^{N^D} \frac{N^D!}{(N^D-k)!N^{N^D-N+k}} \frac{\mathfrak{B}_k}{k!} = 0 \qquad [3.5]$$

where $\mathfrak{B}_k$ is k-th Bernoulli number. Unlike the case $D = 1$, functions with a single global minimum are "infinitely" rare.

3.3.2. *Functions with several global minima*

3.3.2.1. *Dimension $D = 1$*

Let $\mathbb{F}_{m,N}$ be the number of functions of $\mathbb{F}_N$ with m global minima. We have

$$[\![\mathbb{F}_{m,N}]\!] = \binom{N}{m} \sum_{k=1}^{N-m} (N-k)^{N-m}$$

$$= \binom{N}{m} \frac{\mathfrak{B}_{N-m+1}(N-m+1) - \mathfrak{B}_{N-m+1}(0)}{N-m+1}$$

where

$$\nu\left(\mathbb{F}_m\right) = \lim_{N \to \infty} \frac{[\![\mathbb{F}_{m,N}]\!]}{N^N} = \frac{1}{m!\,(e-1)} \qquad [3.6]$$

As can be seen in Figure 3.7, this proportion quickly decreases when m increases, which is fairly logical. Note that we have a formula for shifting from one level to the next:

$$\frac{\nu\left(\mathbb{F}_{m+1}\right)}{\nu\left(\mathbb{F}_m\right)} = \frac{1}{m+1} \qquad [3.7]$$

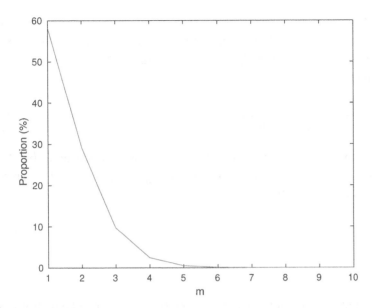

Figure 3.7. *Proportion of functions with m global minima*

3.3.2.2. *Dimension $D \geq 2$*

The general formula is

$$\llbracket \mathbb{F}_{m,N} \rrbracket = \binom{N^D}{m} \sum_{k=1}^{N-m} (N-k)^{N^D-m}$$

$$= \binom{N^D}{m} \frac{\mathfrak{B}_{N^D-m+1}(N-m+1) - \mathfrak{B}_{N^D-m+1}(0)}{N-m+1}$$

and we have

$$\nu\left(\mathbb{F}_{m,D}\right) = \frac{1}{m!} \lim_{N \to \infty} \frac{\mathfrak{B}_{N^D-m+1}(N-m+1)}{(N-m+1) N^{N^{D.-m}}}$$

$$\nu\left(\mathbb{F}_{m,D}\right) = \frac{1}{m!} \lim_{N \to \infty}$$

$$\sum_{k=0}^{N^D-m+1} \frac{N^D!}{(N^D-k)! N^{N^D-N+m-1+k}} \frac{\mathfrak{B}_k}{k!} = 0 \quad [3.8]$$

Considering each m separately, the subset of functions under consideration is negligible, but, of course, the infinite union of all these subsets is $\mathbb{F}$ in its entirety. The interesting point is that equation [3.7] remains valid:

$$\frac{\nu\left(\mathbb{F}_{m+1,D}\right)}{\nu\left(\mathbb{F}_{m,D}\right)} = \frac{1}{m+1} \tag{3.9}$$

Now, consider, on the one hand, $\mathbb{F}_{1,D}$, and on the other hand, the union $\mathbb{F}_{*,D} = \bigcup_{m=2}^{\infty} \mathbb{F}_{m,D}$. Given that $\sum_{m=1}^{\infty} \frac{1}{m!} = e$, we then have the relative proportions:

$$\nu\left(\mathbb{F}_{*,D}\right) = (e-1)\,\nu\left(\mathbb{F}_{1,D}\right) \tag{3.10}$$

3.4. Unimodal functions

Several unimodal functions can be found in many classic test cases. Therefore, they cannot be regarded as being generalist[4], both with respect to algorithms to be tested and problems to be solved. For the latter, we have in effect the following theorem:

THEOREM 3.5.– *Unimodal functions are negligible.*

For a dimension greater than one, we have seen (section 3.3) that functions with a single global minimum are negligible. Since unimodal functions are a subset thereof, they are *a fortiori* themselves negligible. On the contrary, for dimension 1, a specific demonstration is necessary.

Contrary to what one might believe, if a unimodal function is not strictly monotonic, its difficulty (in the NisB sense) is not null. A direct calculation is given in section A.4.

For strictly monotonic functions, the theorem is obvious. In fact, from I_N onto I_N, it is easy to see that there are only two of them

---

4 This is not necessarily a flaw, because it may indeed be desirable to define a specific test case to a certain class of problems, or a certain class of algorithms, but one has to be aware of this fact.

(strictly increasing or strictly decreasing), by application of the pigeonhole principle (see section A.1).

Otherwise, the other unimodal functions are either convex or concave. Let us consider convex ones. There are N possible positions x_{min} for the minimum. For each possible minimum value v_{min}, between 1 and $N - 1$ maximum possible values are between $v_{min} + 1$ and N, and there are $v_{max} - v_{min} - 1$ possible intermediate values (possibly zero) whose positions are in $[1, x_{min}[$. The same goes for positions in $]x_{min}, N]$.

In total, counting symmetric functions twice and taking into account the fact that there are as many concave functions as convex ones, the number of unimodal functions is at most equal to

$$2N \sum_{v_{min}=1}^{N-1} \sum_{v_{max}=v_{min}+1}^{N} \sum_{k=0}^{v_{max}-v_{min}-1} \binom{v_{max} - v_{min} - 1}{k}$$

agreeing that the number of combinations $\binom{m}{0}$ is equal to 1 for every m. The last sum is equal to $2^{v_{max}-v_{min}-1}$. We can then write

$$\frac{[\![\mathbb{F}_l \cap \mathbb{F}_N]\!]}{[\![\mathbb{F}_N]\!]} < \frac{2}{N^{N-1}} \sum_{v_{min}=1}^{N-1} \sum_{v_{max}=v_{min}+1}^{N} 2^{v_{max}-v_{min}-1}$$

$$< \frac{2}{N^{N-1}} \sum_{v_{min}=1}^{N-1} \left(2^{N-v_{min}} - 1\right)$$

$$< \frac{2}{N^{N-1}} \left(2^N - 2 - \frac{N(N-1)}{2}\right)$$

$$\nu(\mathbb{F}_u) \leq \lim_{N \to \infty} \frac{2^{N+1}}{N^{N-1}} = 0$$

This result is not surprising, consolidating the intuition that unimodal functions are very rare, compared to multimodal functions.

4

LandGener

Problems of controllable difficulty can be directly built by defining the positions and sizes of plateaus and basins of attraction of local minima. To this end, I have applied the method described by Algorithm 4.1 (others are obviously possible), in which all the domains of basins and plateaus are D-triangles.

It should be noted that despite the fact that the midpoint has a smaller value than those of the vertices of its D-triangle, this does not guarantee that it will be the local minimum because of the way in which the local basin is defined (polynomial interpolation), even if it is often well the case.

In the Matlab® coding of the LandGener algorithm, I have added a little subtlety so that adjacent basins connect without discontinuity. On the other hand, plateaus may define "cliffs". This is merely for aesthetics, because as such, in dimension 2, quite realistic landscapes can then be obtained. The code is freely available for download. The program possesses a graphical interface, but the various modules (creation, display, calculations of difficulties, etc.) can also be launched at the command line.

1) Place N points in the definition space. To simplify, this space is the D-square $[0, 1]^D$.

2) Option (for small dimension): add the 2^D vertices of the D-square.

3) Define a Delaunay triangulation on the set of these points. Each D-triangle is a domain. This is an interval in dimension 1, a true triangle in dimension 2, a tetrahedron in dimension 3, etc.

4) Indicate which domains support plateaus. The others will support basins.

5) Assign a value to each plateau.

6) For each basin:
  - assign values to the $D + 1$ vertices of the domain, ensuring the continuity for points common to two or more basins;
  - choose a "midpoint" and assign it with a value smaller than those of the vertices of the domain;
  - define a convex unimodal local landscape (a basin) containing the vertices of the domain and the midpoint.

Algorithm 4.1. *LandGener: landscape construction*

4.1. Examples

Figures 4.1 and 4.2 show visible examples of generated landscapes. For dimensions greater than 2, LandGener also allows us to view cross-sections of one or two dimension(s).

REMARK 4.1.– The obvious drawback from imposing that subdomains are polyhedra with $D + 1$ vertices is that their construction requires considering not only N points distributed in the search space but also the 2^D vertices, to ensure that this entire space is "covered". In practice, unless a supercomputer is available, this method cannot be used for large values of dimension D (for example, 2^{30} exceeds one billion).

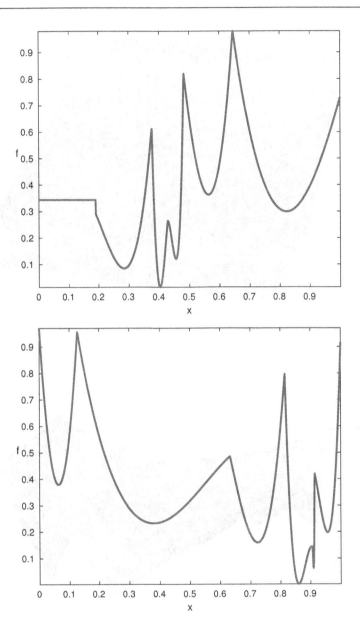

Figure 4.1. *Landscapes* $D = 1$

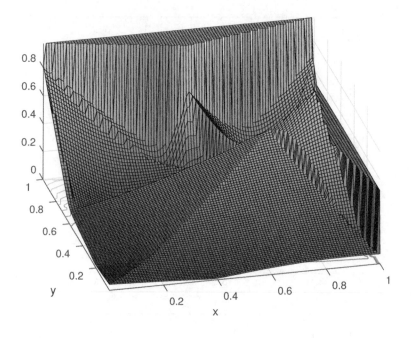

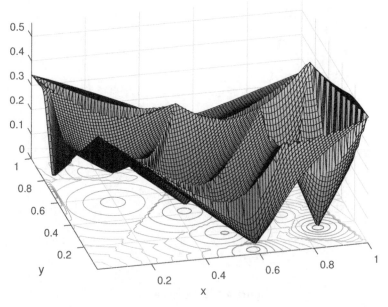

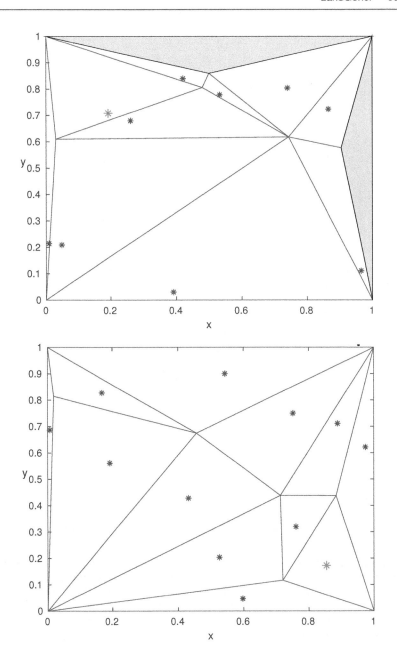

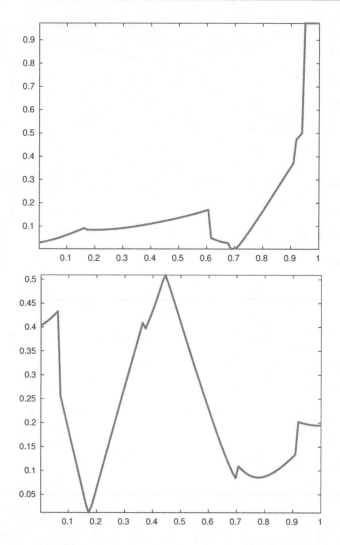

Figure 4.2. *Landscapes* $D = 2$. *The first one has two plateaus. Stars indicate the "midpoints" of basins. The largest indicates that of the lowest value. This is often the global minimum, but not always. The figures at the bottom are 1D cross-sections of 2D landscapes located above, for* $x = 0.2$ *and* $x = 0.85$, *respectively. For a color version of this image, see www.iste.co.uk/clerc/iterative.zip*

For such values of D, a workaround consists of only considering N points, building their triangulation and induced subdomains and imposing that the points outside their union form a "high plateau" (see Figure 4.3) or a set of external "slopes" (Figure 4.4).

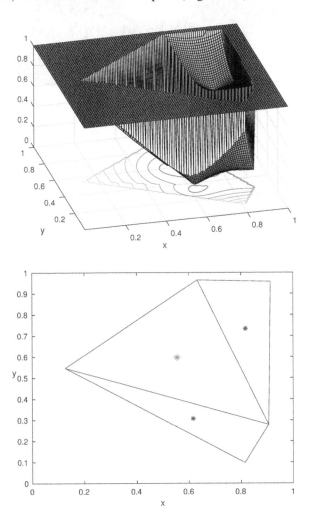

Figure 4.3. *Landscape with external high plateau. The inner points are sufficient to generate it, without taking into account the vertices of the search space. Such landscapes may then be created for even larger values of* D. *For a color version of this image, see www.iste.co.uk/clerc/iterative.zip*

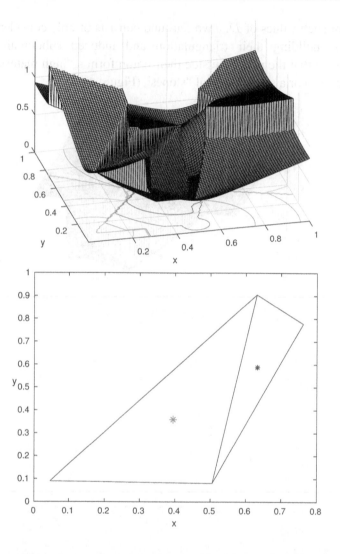

Figure 4.4. *Landscape with external slopes. As for the high plateau, the generation is done using inner points only, without adding the vertices of the search space. For a color version of this image, see www.iste.co.uk/clerc/iterative.zip*

4.2. Generated files

A landscape can be stored in a text file of simple structure, "manually" editable (a few examples are given in section A.13). Its structure for a landscape of dimension D with M domains delimited by S vertices is given in Table 4.1. In general, the smoothing parameter is equal to 1. Different values make the landscape more or less abrupt. Values greater than 2 are to be avoided because they can generate local maxima inside basins due to the polynomial interpolation being used. Therefore, this actually creates basins that were not explicitly expected, which disrupts the calculation of measures of difficulty using the sizes of the domains.

Line	Content
1	$M\ D\ S$ smoothing
2	D vertex coordinates
...	...
$S+1$	D vertex coordinates
$S+2$	D domain midpoint coordinates
...	...
$S+2+M$	D mid-domain coordinates
$S+2+M+1$	domain_type vertex_value vertex_value ... midpoint_value
...	...
$S+2+2M$	domain_type vertex_value vertex_value ... midpoint_value
$S+3+2M$	Likely position of the minimum
$S+4+2M$	Value of this position
$S+5+2M$	Likely value of the maximum

Table 4.1. *Structure of a LandGener landscape text file*

The domain type is encoded by 0 for a plateau and 1 for a basin.

The file can be read by landRead:

```
[x,middle,triangle,structure,smooth,D,xBest,fBest]
=landRead;
```

Then, any position xx can be evaluated by valuex (see section A.12.3):

```
f=valuex(xx, x,middle,triangle, structure,smooth);
```

4.3. Regular landscape

In higher dimensions D, we saw that a decomposition of the definition domain into D-triangles leads to a number of subdomains too large to be addressed in reasonable time on a typical digital computer. The number of subdomains can be considerably reduced using a D-square decomposition.

Better still, even by imposing a few simplifying constraints, landscapes can be defined as having any degree of difficulty greater than or equal to that of a unimodal landscape (arbitrarily defined, let us recall, by the parameter δ_{uni}, which is appropriate to set to $\frac{1}{2}$).

We reuse the formulas of section 2.6 defining the measure δ_0:

$$\text{and} \quad \begin{cases} \delta = \frac{1}{s_{i*}} + \sum_{i \neq i*} s_i \frac{f_{max} - f_{i*}}{f_i - f_{i*}} \\ \delta_0 = 1 - \frac{1}{\sqrt{\delta} + \frac{\delta_{uni}}{1 - \delta_{uni}}} \end{cases}$$

We impose the following equalities, where ν is the number of domains:

– $s_{i*} = s_i = s$ and $\nu s = 1$. The domains are all the same size and the whole set covers the standard search space.

– $f_{max} = 1$ and $f_{i*} = 0$. The space of values is normalized in $[0, 1]$.

– $f_i = f < 1$. All local minima have the same value.

Taking into account that $\nu s = 1$ and simplifying, with $\delta_{uni} = \frac{1}{2}$, we then get

$$\delta_0 = 1 - \frac{1}{1 + \sqrt{\frac{1}{s} + s\frac{\nu - 1}{f}}} = 1 - \frac{1}{1 + \sqrt{\nu + \frac{\nu - 1}{\nu f}}} \qquad [4.1]$$

It can be deduced, for example, that with two domains, δ_0 cannot be smaller than $1 - \frac{1}{1 + \sqrt{2}} \simeq 0.586$.

For a single domain, we have $\delta_0 = \frac{1}{2}$. Note that this is also valid for any unimodal landscape, since it can be seen as regular as defined above. This is the case of the landscape P_0 of Table 2.1. More generally, Figure 4.5 gives the possible minimal and maximal values of δ_0, making f tend to 1 or 0. There is a little subtlety in the interpretation. In fact, when f tends to zero, which is the value of the global minimum, the user can consider that every position of the minima is an acceptable solution and that, therefore, the problem becomes easier. In fact, it is considered here that this is a unique position that must be found (that of the global minimum) and not a value. Within this context, the mere presence of a single local basin very similar to the global basin thus indeed increases the difficulty.

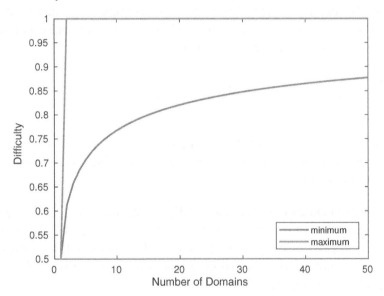

Figure 4.5. *Regular landscapes. Possible minimal and maximal difficulty δ_0 according to the number of domains. For a color version of this image, see www.iste.co.uk/clerc/iterative.zip*

The actual construction in itself could be achieved as a special case of the general algorithm 4.1:

– define a mesh in the search space $[0, 1]^D$ in identical D-squares, of edge a. If D is too large, the search space cannot be completely covered and supplemented with a high plateau or external slopes (see 4.1);

– decompose each D-square into $D!$ D-triangles of same size;

– assign the same value f less than 1 to the center of gravity of each D-triangle.

Then, continue as from point 4 of Algorithm 4.1.

However, again, this method is acceptable only for small dimensions. Even if it requires defining a regular landscape, it is clearly more economical not to break down the D-squares into D-triangles. They then form a^{-D} identical domains, upon which it is easy to define a local landscape, for example, by means of a second-degree polynomial. Each local landscape (sub-landscape) can be calculated by a formula as follows:

$$f\left(x\right) = \alpha + \left(1 - \alpha\right) \sum_{d=1}^{D} \left(x_d - m_d\right)^2$$

where m is the center of the D-square, with $0 < \alpha < 1$. For one of the sub-landscapes, we actually choose $\alpha = 0$, which will thus be the global minimum.

Such a landscape, which can be called multi-paraboloid, is presented in Figure 4.6. However, a wide range of theoretical problems can be obtained, just by changing the number of D-squares and the common value of minima, as indicated by equation [4.1], which is graphically represented by Figure 4.7.

It should be noted that increasing the number of domains ν is tantamount to decreasing the relative size of the global basin, which is $\frac{1}{\nu-1}$. It is thus intuitively normal that difficulty increases.

It is also possible to give different values to local minima and to replace certain paraboloids by plateaus, as in Figure 4.8. For some optimizers, especially those confused by plateaus, it may increase the perceived difficulty.

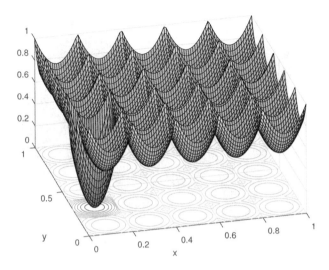

Figure 4.6. *Multi-paraboloid with local minima of the same value. For a color version of this image, see www.iste.co.uk/clerc/iterative.zip*

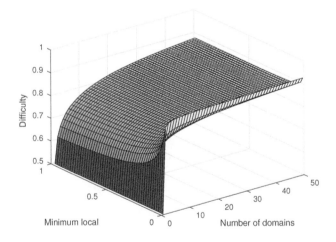

Figure 4.7. *Difficulty δ_0 of a regular landscape with local minima as common values. When the latter is very close to zero (the global minimum), it significantly increases difficulty, but otherwise has little impact. For a color version of this image, see www.iste.co.uk/clerc/iterative.zip*

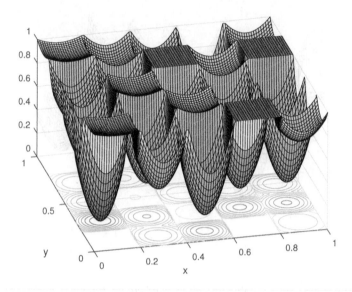

Figure 4.8. *Multi-paraboloid with local minima and plateaus. For a color version of this image, see www.iste.co.uk/clerc/iterative.zip*

Test Cases

In Chapter 3, we defined a possible typology of every function (or landscape). Given that a test case comprises a restricted number of functions, its structure cannot be completely in accordance with this typology. Choices will have to be made as well as compromises that bias the test case.

5.1. Structure of a representative test case

As we have seen, unimodal functions are negligible and, therefore, the test case should not include any. In practice, however, it is useful to have at least one, to ensure that the optimizer to be tested is capable of finding the minimum in a simple case. It should be noted that, from a certain point of view, all unimodal functions are equivalent (see section A.6).

In addition, except in dimension 1, the proportion of functions with m global minima should be zero for any m, which is obviously impossible with a limited test case. A possible compromise could be a case including a proportion τ_1 of functions with a single global minimum, a proportion $\tau_2 \simeq \frac{\tau_1}{2!}$ of functions with two global minima and so on up to a given value of m, using formula [3.9].

The constraint is that $\sum_{m=1}^{M} \tau_m = 100\%$. In fact, this tradeoff is also valid for the first dimension, except that, in this case, it is not necessary to impose an arbitrary non-zero value for τ_1, because we can use the theoretical value (58%).

Type of function	Proportion for $D = 1$	Proportion for $D > 1$
Unimodal	0%	0%
With plateau(s)	$1 - e^{-1} \simeq 63\%$	$1 - e^{-2^D} \simeq 100\%$
Deceptive >	50%	50% (experimental)
One global minimum	58%	$\tau_1 = 0\%$
Several global minima	42%	$\tau_* = 100\%$

Table 5.1. *Theoretical typology of every function*

Regarding plateaus, it can be noted that on a digital computer, a function has almost always at least a small one. Let ε be the machine epsilon of the computer and D be the dimension of the definition space.

We assume that there are $D + 1$ points (x_i, x_j) such that $\|x_i, x_j\| \leq D\varepsilon$ and for which the function definition implies $|f(x_i) - f(x_j)| < \varepsilon$. The computer then assigns the same value to these "adjacent" points, which thus form a mini-plateau.

Type of function	Proportion for $D = 1$	Proportion for $D > 1$
Unimodal	$\frac{1}{F}\%$	$\frac{1}{F}\%$
Deceptive	50%	50%
1 global minimum	$\tau_1 = 58\%$	τ_1 (arbitrary)
2 global minima	29%	$\frac{\tau_1}{2}$
3 global minima	10%	$\frac{\tau_1}{3!}$
3 global minima	2.4%	$\frac{\tau_1}{4}$
5 global minima	0.5%	$\frac{\tau_1}{5}$
6 global minima	0.1%	$\frac{\tau_1}{6!}$

Table 5.2. *Compromise for a test case of F functions*

We can then propose a reasonable structure for a representative test case (see Table 5.2). In order to build such a test case, we need deceptive functions, but which are not too "monstrous", expecting that similar features exist in the real world. Examples of such functions are given in section A.7.

Let us see now if the choice of functions of two conventional test cases is somewhat compatible with the proposed structure.

Code	Name	Difficulty $\delta^*_{\neg NisB}$
1	*Shifted Sphere Function*	0
2	*Shifted Schwefel's Problem 1.2*	0.413
3	*Shifted Rotated High Conditioned Elliptic Function*	0.384
4	*Shifted Schwefel's Problem 1.2 with Noise in Fitness*	0.419
5	*Schwefel's Problem 2.6 with Global Optimum on Bounds*	0.220
6	*Shifted Rosenbrock's Function*	0.118
7	*Shifted Rotated Griewank's Function without Bounds*	0.128
8	*Shifted Rotated Ackley's Function with Global Optimum on Bounds*	*0.501*
9	*Shifted Rastrigin's Function*	0.139
10	*Shifted Rotated Rastrigin's Function*	0.144
11	*Shifted Rotated Weierstrass Function*	*0.500*
12	*Schwefel's Problem 2.13*	*0.497*
13	*Expanded Extended Griewank's plus Rosenbrock's Function (F8F2)*	0.289
14	*Shifted Rotated Expanded Scaffer's F6*	*0.503*
15	*Hybrid Composition Function*	0.402
16	*Rotated Hybrid Composition Function*	0.407
17	*Rotated Hybrid Composition Function with Noise in Fitness*	0.419
18	*Rotated Hybrid Composition Function*	**0.629**
19	*Rotated Hybrid Composition Function with a Narrow Basin for the Global*	**0.633**
20	*Rotated Hybrid Composition Function with the Global Optimum on the Bound*	**0.611**
21	*Rotated Hybrid Composition Function*	**0.543**
22	*Rotated Hybrid Composition Function with High Condition Number Matrix*	**0.561**
23	*Non-Continuous Rotated Hybrid Composition Function*	**0.543**
24	*Rotated Hybrid Composition Function*	0.480
25	*Rotated Hybrid Composition Function without Bounds*	0.480

Table 5.3. *CEC 2005 test case. Difficulty for dimension $D = 10$*

5.2. CEC 2005

In this test case, functions are completely artificial (Suganthan *et al.* 2005), which means that their global minimum is perfectly known. The degree of difficulty in the sense $\delta^*_{\neg NisB}$ is an experimental estimate. For each function, the number of generated triplets is large enough to "stabilize" its value to the third decimal place.

As we can see, most functions are reliable. Four are neutral slightly deceptive or (8, 11, 12, 14), assuming that the estimate is sufficiently accurate.

As it could be expected, the *Sphere* function is the easiest and certain hybrid functions are clearly deceptive. Not all of them, but 15, 16, 17, 24 and 25 are reliable and are even of rather low difficulty for the first three.

For this test case, the typology is given in Table 5.4. There are clearly too many unimodal functions, knowing that, in theory, these are "infinitely" rare. On the other hand, the lack of functions with important plateaus is obvious.

Functions	Proportion type for $D > 1$
Unimodal	20 %
With plateau(s)	0 %
Neutral	12 %
Deceptive	24 %
One single global minimum	$\tau_1 = 100\%$
Several global minima	$\tau_* = 0\%$

Table 5.4. *Typology of the CEC 2005 test case*

5.3. CEC 2011

Here, the functions are supposed to model real problems (Das and Suganthan 2011). It should be noted that there is an error in the Matlab® code for functions 5 and 6 (*Tersoff potential Si(B) and Si(C)*), and some positions are not evaluated because of too large intermediate values during the calculation (and therefore considered to be infinite). Hence, I have changed the code so that, in this case, a high value be affected as well as, in addition, slightly random to avoid the artificial creation of plateaus.

Code	Name	Dimension	Difficulty $\delta^*_{\neg NisB}$
1	*Parameter Estimation for Frequency-Modulated (FM) Sound Waves*	6	0.458
2	*Lennard-Jones Potential Problem*	30	**0.973**
3	*The Bifunctional Catalyst Blend Optimal Control Problem*	1	0.046
4	*Optimal Control of a Non-Linear Stirred Tank Reactor*	1	0.246
5	*Tersoff Potential for model Si (B)*	30	0.368 ?
6	*Tersoff Potential for model Si (C)*	30	0.490 ?
7	*Spread Spectrum Radar Polyphase Code Design*	20	**0.545**
8	*Transmission Network Expansion Planning (TNEP) Problem*	7	0.423
9	*Large Scale Transmission Pricing Problem*	126	0.506 ?
10	*Circular Antenna Array Design Problem*	12	0.442
11.1	*Dynamic Economic Dispatch (DED) Instance 1*	120	0.395 ?
11.2	*DED Instance 2*	216	0.272 ?
11.3	*Economic Load Dispatch (ELD) Instance 1*	6	0.309
11.4	*ELD Instance 2*	13	0.378
11.5	*ELD Instance 3*	15	0.186 ?
11.6	*ELD Instance 4*	40	**0.562**
11.7	*ELD Instance 5*	140	?
11.8	*Hydrothermal Scheduling Instance 1*	96	?
11.9	*Hydrothermal Scheduling Instance 2*	96	?
12	*Messenger: Spacecraft Trajectory Optimization Problem*	26	0.475
13	*Cassini 2: Spacecraft Trajectory Optimization Problem*	22	0.463

Table 5.5. *CEC 2011 test case. Difficulties in problems. Some are deceptive, probably under-evaluated, and when the position of the global minimum is too poorly known (11.7, 11.8, 11.9), the estimated difficulty is questionable*

To build Table 5.5, this value is given by $10^{10} + U(0,1)$, where $U(0,1)$ is a realization of the uniform random variable in $[0,1]$.

Moreover, in most cases, the global minimum is not known with certainty. I have then used the best solution that I could find (as of June 2018), either in publications or by executing optimization algorithms[1].

For this test case, the typology is given in Table 5.6. Because of symmetries, the Lennard-Jones problem admits several global minima. The measure $\delta^*_{\neg NisB}$ somewhat overestimates its difficulty, because it assumes the search for a given global minimum.

Function type	Proportion
Unimodal	0 %
With plateau(s)	0 %
Neutral	8 %
Deceptive	3 %
One single global minimum	$\tau_1 = 92\%$
Several global minima	$\tau_* = 8\%$

Table 5.6. *Typology of the CEC 2011 test case*

On the one hand, there are no unimodal functions, which is consistent with the theoretical typology, but on the other hand, there are not enough deceptive functions. Concerning real problems, it remains nevertheless an open question. Perhaps, in fact, by examining a large body of such problems, one would find that most are reliable.

In addition, there should be theoretically about 42% of functions with several global minima, but, in fact, the great majority of problems have only one single global minimum. But here again, this corresponds perhaps to problems encountered in reality.

---

1 Published articles give the values of the solutions found by any particular algorithm, but almost never the solutions themselves, which is nonetheless crucial information for a practitioner.

6

Difficulty vs Dimension

Expressions such as "Let us study the same problem in different dimensions" can sometimes be seen. This is very often misleading, because even if landscapes are defined by formulae that are mathematically identical with the dimension as the only variable parameter, their structures are usually different. We shall examine two examples for which it is clearly the case and, on the contrary, two examples in which the structure is preserved when the dimension increases.

6.1. Rosenbrock function

The landscape is defined by the function f:

$$f(x_1, \ldots, x_D) = \sum_{d=1}^{D-1} \left[(1 - x_d)^2 + k \left(x_{d+1} - x_d^2 \right)^2 \right] \qquad [6.1]$$

with in general $k = 100$. The problem is not separable. It is unimodal for $D \leq 3$ and the minimum is at point $(1, \ldots, 1)$, therefore on a diagonal of the search space. However, it becomes bimodal for $4 \leq D \leq 7$, where the second (local) minimum is variable according to the value of D. Thereby, it can not be said that this is the "same problem" in different dimensions. A detailed study of this behavior is given in Shang and Qiu (2006).

6.2. Griewank function

It is defined by

$$f(x) = 1 + \sum_{d=1}^{D} \frac{x_d^2}{4000} - \prod_{d=1}^{D} \cos\left(\frac{x_d}{\sqrt{d}}\right)$$

Its minimum is at the origin of coordinates and is equal to zero.

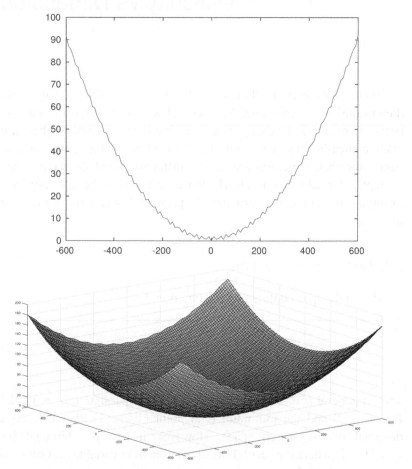

Figure 6.1. *The Griewank function in dimensions 1 and 2. For a color version of this image, see www.iste.co.uk/clerc/iterative.zip*

The number of local minima increases exponentially with the dimension and yet, in a counterintuitive manner, it is increasingly easier to find the global minimum. The interested reader could study the explanation given in (Locatelli 2003). In short, the basins of attraction of local minima become increasingly numerous as well as increasingly smaller. It is then all the more easy for an iterative optimizer to escape therefrom. In fact, the landscape tends towards that of a unimodal function with increasingly more reduced fluctuations. Here again, it is improper to refer to the "same problem" in different dimensions.

Meanwhile, we shall see what information can be obtained from some of our measures of difficulty estimated by the Monte Carlo method. Table 6.1 shows that only the measure $\delta^*_{\neg NisB}$ clearly reflects the decreasing difficulty according to the dimension, such as it is perceived by most optimizers. Remember that it is established considering position triplets, of which one is the global minimum (see section 2.7).

Dimension	$\delta^*_{\neg NisB}$	$\delta_{\neg NisB}$	δ_r, threshold 0.001
1	0.26	0.363	0.9996
2	0.14	0.348	$\simeq 1$
3	0.08	0.363	$\simeq 1$
4	0.047	0.365	$\simeq 1$
10	0.003	0.388	$\simeq 1$

Table 6.1. *Estimated difficulties for the Griewank function*

6.3. Example of the normalized paraboloid

Assume that we know how to define a series of landscapes $P(D)$ of increasing dimension D and all sharing the same structure (at least at level 4, see Chapter 1). For example, consider the normalized paraboloid (Figure 6.2), defined on $[0, 1]^D$, which is unimodal in any dimension.

$$f\left(x\right) = \frac{4}{D}\sum_{d=1}^{D}\left(x_d - \frac{1}{2}\right)^2$$

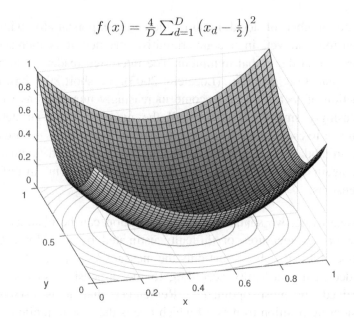

Figure 6.2. *Normalized paraboloid. Maximum 1, minimum 0 in*
$\left(\frac{1}{2}, \ldots, \frac{1}{2}\right)$. *For a color version of this image, see*
www.iste.co.uk/clerc/iterative.zip

Experimentally, the evolution of the perceived difficulty can be found according to D for some optimizers based on different principles (GA-MPC, SAMODE, SPSO 2011, APS). The necessary effort E simply has to be found – as the number of evaluations – to obtain, for example, a value at most equal to $\varepsilon = 0.001$ with a success rate of at least $p = 80\%$. The evolution curves are given in Figure 6.3 for dimensions 1 to 15.

For APS and SPSO 2011 (Clerc 2012, Zambrano-Bigiarini *et al.* 2013), a population of 12 agents can be enough[1]. In fact, even for

---

1 For this test, it is necessary to slightly change APS. In fact, in general, during initialization it samples the center of the search space with a given probability. As in our example, it is precisely the solution point, it thus always finds it with at least this probability, regardless of the dimension. To avoid this favorable bias, the initialization is here entirely randomly made, according to a uniform distribution.

dimension 15, obtaining such a high success rate is quite easily possible.

For GA-MPC, as soon as the dimension is larger than 4 or 5, this is impossible with a small population, even when considerably increasing the effort. The algorithm stagnates on probabilities lower than 80%. It is necessary to utilize a population of 90, which, on the other hand, also distorts comparisons for small dimensions, because the probabilities of success are then, on the contrary, far greater than p. Furthermore, the efforts found are multiples of the population, because the algorithm always completes a full iteration, even when an acceptable solution has already been found during the iteration in progress.

For SAMODE, the Matlab® code executes only[2] for populations of the $4k$ form, with $k \geq 20$.

Figures 6.3 also present models originating from simplistic reasoning. To establish these models, it is admitted that effort E is an increasing function of D. Then, it can be assumed that the larger the dimension, the less its increase will affect that of the effort. However, it can also be considered that the addition of a dimension increases in fact the necessary effort of a constant value. Furthermore, there is at least one situation where this is guaranteed: when the problem is separable and when the optimizer considers every dimension independently.

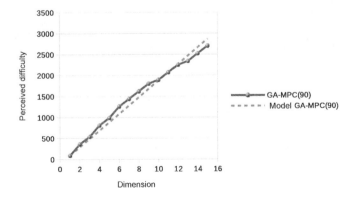

---

2 And again, I had to correct the code because in some cases it engaged in an infinite *while* loop.

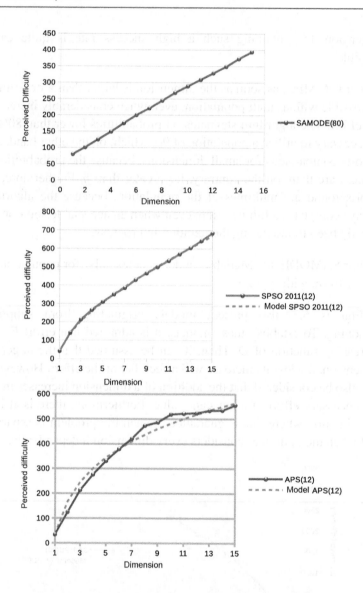

Figure 6.3. *Normalized paraboloid. Perceived difficulty versus dimension. The log-linear mixed model can be applied to every case, with extremes (purely linear for SAMODE, almost entirely logarithmic for APS)*

Rather than making a choice between the two ideas, we try a discrete differential formula combining them:

$$\Delta E = \left(\frac{a}{D} + b \right) \Delta D \qquad\qquad [6.2]$$

The result is a logarithmic + linear mixed model (called mixed log-linear, to simplify, or even just mixed model if the context does not allow any confusion):

$$E\left(D\right) = E\left(1\right) + a \ln\left(D\right) + bD \qquad\qquad [6.3]$$

The interesting point is that, despite its rudimentary nature, it is apparent this mixed model applies very well. In fact, for algorithms that operate from one dimension to another, the linear part is even sufficient (coefficient b nearly zero). On the contrary, for those that work more generally (SPSO 2011 with hyperspheres and APS with triplets of points), the logarithmic part is necessary. For APS, it is even widely predominant ($a = 188.6$ and $b = 1.24$).

6.4. Normalized bi-paraboloid

Is the mixed model seen above still suitable for more complicated landscapes?

We should already note that, for most agent population-based iterative optimizers, after a certain number of iterations, all agents can be found in the same basin of attraction. The landscape "seen" by the optimizer then becomes unimodal, as in the previous example.

Thus, in practice, except for the unimodal case, it is rare to have a series of landscapes of increasing dimensions and the same structure. It is also not so easy to artificially build them because it is necessary to maintain the same distance between maximum and minimum, the same number of domains, with same sizes and same values of local minima. Figure 6.4 however provides an example thereof, from which we are going to study the behavior of the optimizers used in the previous case.

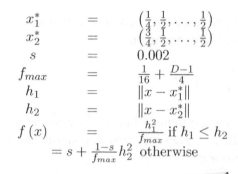

$$
\begin{aligned}
x_1^* &= \left(\tfrac{1}{4}, \tfrac{1}{2}, \ldots, \tfrac{1}{2}\right) \\
x_2^* &= \left(\tfrac{3}{4}, \tfrac{1}{2}, \ldots, \tfrac{1}{2}\right) \\
s &= 0.002 \\
f_{max} &= \tfrac{1}{16} + \tfrac{D-1}{4} \\
h_1 &= \|x - x_1^*\| \\
h_2 &= \|x - x_2^*\| \\
f(x) &= \tfrac{h_1^2}{f_{max}} \text{ if } h_1 \leq h_2 \\
&= s + \tfrac{1-s}{f_{max}} h_2^2 \text{ otherwise}
\end{aligned}
$$

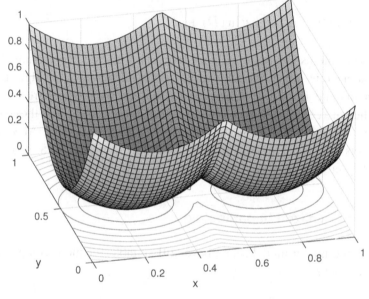

Figure 6.4. *Normalized bi-paraboloid. In any dimension, the global minimum 0 is at x_1^* and the local minimum s is at x_2^*. For a color version of this image, see www.iste.co.uk/clerc/iterative.zip*

Again, we shall look for the effort E necessary to obtain a value at most equal to $\varepsilon = 0.001$ with a success rate at the least of $p = 80\%$. Note that the effort increases with dimension D if only we have $\varepsilon < s$. Otherwise, the whole region around the local minimum becomes acceptable and, suddenly, the effort required decreases abruptly.

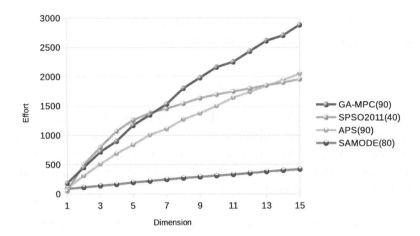

Figure 6.5. *Normalized bi-paraboloid. Perceived difficulty (required effort) versus dimension. The four curves are very well represented by the log-linear mixed model. For a color version of this image, see www.iste.co.uk/clerc/iterative.zip*

Figure 6.5 requires a few comments:

– to obtain it, recommended population sizes have been used in source codes. This was already the case for GA-MPC and SAMODE in the previous example, but in this one, imposing a size of 12 for SPSO 2011 and APS is no longer suitable and leads to excessive efforts (typically on the order of 10,000 for dimension 15);

– during experiments, it has appeared that success rates could be highly variable from one sequence of executions to another. Thereby, every effort value is the one that, on average on five sequences of a thousand executions, gives the desired success rate (80%);

– the curves of mixed models are not represented to allow the figure to be easily read, but again, they practically merge with real curves, except for GA-MPC, for which the real curve presents small shifts. As already indicated, this is due to the fact that for this optimizer, efforts are necessarily multiples of 90;

– this is not the subject of this study, but it should be noted that, with this problem, SAMODE is by far the most effective. The reason is that it is much more "aggressive" in intensifying the search around a promising position. This is an advantage here and it would be a disadvantage for a landscape with many local minima.

6.5. Difficulty δ_0 and dimension

It is not advisable to directly compare the difficulties δ_0 of landscapes of different dimensions. Nevertheless, this is sometimes necessary. We can then attempt to apply a model similar to the one seen above. However, it must be done before normalization and, therefore, on δ, as defined in section 2.6.

If we are able to calculate the difficulty $\delta(1)$ of $P(1)$, the results seen above suggest that the difficulty in dimension D can be estimated by a formula such as

$$\delta(D) = \langle b(D-1) + a\ln(D) + \delta(1) \rangle \qquad [6.4]$$

and only then apply an increasing bijective normalization formula on $[0, 1]$. Unfortunately, the determination of the coefficients a and b is not trivial. In practice, it is necessary to find the experimental values of the difficulty perceived for three or four values of D and then to infer therefrom the most suitable values for the extrapolation–interpolation formula [6.4].

7

Exploitation and Exploration vs Difficulty

Essentially, the sampling strategies of an optimizer are responsible for the latter assuming whether a problem is easy or difficult. For example, for a purely greedy algorithm (see section A.11), a unimodal problem is very easy and a multimodal problem is very difficult as soon as the basin of attraction of the global minimum is significantly smaller than that of a local minimum.

The classic mantra that can be found in many articles and books is that there must be a "balance" between exploitation and exploration (sometimes referred to as intensification and diversification). As such, definitions sufficiently accurate to calculate these two quantities and observe the evolution of their ratio during the iterations are rarely given (see however Naudts *et al.* (1999) and Chen *et al.* (2009))

To clearly bring forward the influence of the exploitation/exploration ratio, we shall see:

– rigorous definitions of these two concepts, making it possible to measure them;

– then, in the next chapter, a very simple optimizer, which will explicitly use an exploitation method, an exploration method and an evolution strategy of their ratio.

7.1. Exploitation, an incomplete definition

In Clerc (2014), I proposed a formalization of exploitation in the case of particle swarm optimization (PSO), which maintains in permanence a list of "good" positions (swarm-memory). It is revisited here word for word in the box below and it is called Method 0.

For each dimension d, the coordinates of the "good" memorized positions $p_j(t)$ are classified in ascending order. We then have

$$x_{min,d} \leq p_{\alpha_d(1),d}(t) \leq \ldots \leq p_{\alpha_d(S),d} \leq x_{max,d}$$

By convention, we will denote $p_{\alpha_d(0),d} = x_{min,d}$ and $p_{\alpha_d(S+1),d} = x_{max,d}$. We shall say that $x_i(t+1)$ is an exploitation point around $p_j(t)$ if, for any dimension d, if $\alpha_d(k) = j$ then

$$p_{j,d}(t) - \delta\left(p_{j,d}(t) - p_{\alpha(k-1),d}(t)\right) \leq x_{i,d}(t+1)$$

$$\leq p_{j,d}(t) + \delta\left(p_{\alpha(k+1),d}(t) - p_{j,d}(t)\right)$$

where δ is a coefficient less than $1/2$ (typically $1/3$).

Box 7.1. *Exploitation, method 0 (Clerc 2014)*

However, this definition is affected by several weaknesses:

– it is not very intuitive;

– it is not associated with a definition of exploration;

– it generates an exploitation domain smaller than necessary, because it takes into account the coordinates of every point, according to each dimension (see, for example, Figure 7.1);

– exploitation domain is generally not a D-square but a D-rectangle, even when the search space has been normalized precisely not to give priority to any direction.

Regarding the second default, we could state that any sampling of points that is not of exploitation is, by definition, of exploration. However, almost every iterative optimizer is only capable of remembering a small number of positions and "forgets" those that seemed uninteresting.

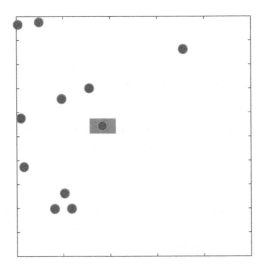

Figure 7.1. *With method 0, the exploitation domain (a D-rectangle) is often smaller than necessary. In addition, it is not a D-square, which for no reason gives preference to certain directions*

As a result, by believing that it is doing exploration in the search space, it is nevertheless able to sample very close to a position already seen and evaluated but forgotten, and therefore it is in fact able to do exploitation.

Hence, there is a need for better definitions.

7.2. Rigorous definitions

There are two prerequisites:

– because we shall use distances, it is necessary that the search space be normalized as a D-cube (for example, $[0, 1]^D$);

– to prevent doing exploitation while believing it is doing exploration, it is necessary to keep in memory the list of all sampled positions.

Then, the first possible definition of exploitation around position i is the following:

> – find, in the list, the position j such that $r = distance\,(i,j)$ is minimal;
>
> – consider the D-sphere $S\,(i, \alpha r)$ of center i and radius αr with $\alpha < 1$. This is the exploitation domain;
>
> – sample in S;
>
> – if the point is outside the search space, bring back to the boundary (0 or 1) the erroneous coordinates.

Box 7.2. *Exploitation, method 1*

Sampling can be done according to any probability distribution law. One that seems to give quite good results is a "bell" distribution, centered in i and of support S.

The advantage of this method is that the average radius of exploitation domains decreases as the search progresses because it is easy to see that it is of the order of $N^{1/D}$, where N is the number of sampled points.

The disadvantage is that when D increases, the volume of S decreases, relative to that of the circumscribed D-cube, with the ratio of both quickly tending towards zero.

In practice, a corrective coefficient can then be applied to the radius; typically r can be replaced by βr with

$$\beta = \frac{2}{\sqrt{\pi}}\Gamma\left(\frac{D}{2}+1\right)^{\frac{1}{D}}$$

so that the volume of S is equal to the volume of the D-cube $[0, 2\alpha r]^D$. This is also how, in SPSO 2011 (Clerc 2012, Zambrano-Bigiarini *et al.* 2013), local search is achieved around the best-known position.

However, as a result, the definition is less rigorous, because an exploitation domain can then contain already-known positions other than its center. Hence the idea of a definition directly from D-cubes, but without the third flaw of method 0:

– start from the D-sphere $S\left(i, \alpha r\right)$ of the previous method;

– consider its circumscribed D-cube C_i;

– sample in C_i. Here again, sampling can be done following several methods;

– if the point is outside the research space, bring to the boundary (0 or 1) the erroneous coordinates.

Box 7.3. *Exploitation, method 2*

At every instant, there are N possible exploitation domains. Which one should be used? Here are some possible strategies:

1) the one around the best point;

2) the one around one of the k best points, randomly chosen in a uniform manner;

3) the one around one of the k best points, randomly chosen according to a decreasing probability with the value of the point.

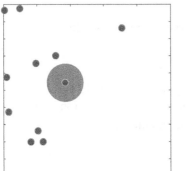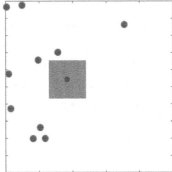

Figure 7.2. *Two definitions of exploitation, by D-sphere and by D-cube*

Contrary to intuition, which would suggest the last strategy, experimentally, it seems that strategy 2 is the most robust in a sufficiently diversified test case.

Once the operation is well defined and because the list of all sampled points has been set aside, the definition of exploration is immediate: it is merely the logical negation of exploitation, that is, considering the union of all the domains of exploitation (*D*-spheres for method 1 or *D*-cubes for method 2) centered on the points in the list and then sampling outside this set.

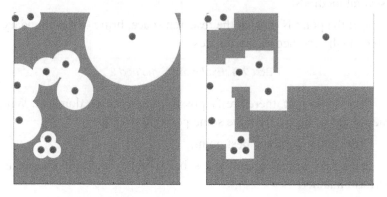

Figure 7.3. *Two definitions of exploration,*
by the logical negation of operation

A possible implementation is more precisely as follows:

– randomly choose a point in $[0, 1]^D$;

– consider the closest known point and test if, by chance, the chosen point belongs to its domain of exploitation, either the *D*-sphere (method 1) or the *D*-cube (method 2);

– if it does, repeat.

Box 7.4. *Random exploration, methods 1 and 2, using loops of attempts*

This process is not quite the logical negation of exploitation. In fact, we should consider not only the closest point but also every point. The computational time then quickly becomes prohibitive for a non-significant gain of efficiency as soon as its dimension is greater than 1.

In dimension 1, in addition, the probability of finding by chance one point that is not in any domain of exploitation decreases very quickly with this number of points. As a result, the number of attempts increases so much that the process becomes particularly slow. This second reason justifies, in practice, the need for a specific method, for example, the following:

– sort by ascending order the list of known positions;

– if necessary, add 0 before the first element and 1 after the last element;

– in this new list, take the middle of the larger interval.

Box 7.5. *Deterministic exploration in dimension 1*

A more sophisticated method requires sub-optimization. For example, one can use SunnySpell, which I had developed in 2005 for Tribes (Clerc 2003, Clerc 2005, Cooren *et al.* 2008), a variant of PSO. It consists of ensuring that the new point is as far as possible from both the boundaries of the search space and already-known points. This sub-optimization does not need to be very accurate. The potential function to be minimized can be rudimentary (see box below) and a single run is enough. For each of the two exploration points shown in Figure 7.4, it is APS that was used, with a population of 6 and a budget of 100 evaluations. For the source code, see section A.12.2.

We have the points $E = \{X_1, X_2, \ldots, X_N\}$ already sampled in the search space $I_D = [0, 1]^D$, with $X_i = (x_{i,1}, x_{i,2}, \ldots, x_{i,D})$.

We are looking for X^*, the point $X = (x_1, x_2, \ldots, x_D)$ that minimizes the sum of two repulsion functions h_1 and h_2, one with respect to the "walls" of I_D, the other with respect to E:

$$h_1 = \frac{1}{\min_{d=1}^{D} \min\left(x_d^{\beta}, (1-x_d)^{\beta}\right)}$$

$$h_2 = \frac{1}{\min\|X^* - X_d\|^{\beta}}$$

[7.1]

The parameter β is only here to accentuate the differences in potential. It is typically equal to 0.1. Figure 7.5 shows a landscape of this potential on 10 known points. Its minimum provides a point of exploration.

Other functions can obviously be used. Therefore, h_1 can be replaced by an increasing function h_3 of the distance from x^* to the center of I_D, for example, this distance itself. This simulates an attraction by this center, which is theoretically tantamount to a repulsion by the "walls". However, in practice, the landscape of $h3 + h1$ has local minima at the center of I_D and at its summits, from which it is difficult to escape. The optimizer will then give too easily, for example, $X^* = (0, 0, \ldots, 0)$ or $\left(\frac{1}{2}, \frac{1}{2}, \ldots, \frac{1}{2}\right)$.

Box 7.6. SunnySpell *exploration*

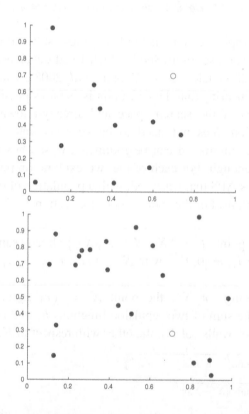

Figure 7.4. *Exploration by* SunnySpell. *The sub-optimizations have been made with APS (population of 6, budget of 100 evaluations, one single run)*

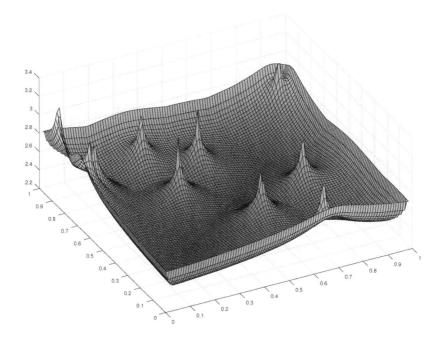

Figure 7.5. *A SunnySpell landscape on 10 already sampled points. Its global minimum is normally a good point of exploration, but even some local minima are acceptable. For a color version of this image, see www.iste.co.uk/clerc/iterative.zip*

An interesting question is the following: is it still possible to find an exploration point? Or, expressed differently, is it possible that the set of exploitation domains completely covers the search space? The answer is positive, particularly if these domains are D-squares and D is small. The risk is however low and, primarily, temporary. Indeed, adding a new point (obviously of exploitation) destroyed some D-squares and replaced them with others, which, for their part, are no longer a covering (see Figure 7.6).

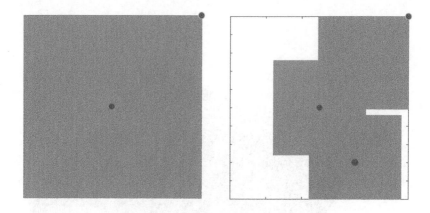

Figure 7.6. *At the visible point on the left-hand side, no exploration is possible, and the D-squares cover the search space. Nonetheless, adding an exploitation point recreates "free space". For a color version of this image, see www.iste.co.uk/clerc/iterative.zip*

7.3. Balance profile

Nevertheless, theoretically there is a little constraint. Let $n_{exploit}(t)$ (resp. $n_{explored}(t)$) be the number of points that have been sampled as exploitation (resp. exploration). We define the balance profile

$$\underline{\Omega}(t) = \frac{n_{exploit}(t)}{n_{explor}(t)} \qquad [7.2]$$

where t is the number of iterations. We have the following small theorem.

THEOREM 7.1.– *On a digital computer and if sampling is carried out without duplicates, the balance profile eventually increases towards a constant.*

Here, "without duplicates" means that no point is sampled more than once. The proof is trivial. In fact, the number of points N of the search space is finite (typically, something like 2^{KD}, where K is the number of bits). Consequently, as the number of sampled points increases and they are assumed to all be different, then sooner or later, the set of their exploitation domains will cover the search space. From a certain t_1, only exploitation points will therefore remain and the balance ratio becomes

$$\underline{\Omega}(t) = \frac{n_{exploit}(t_1) + t - t_1}{n_{explor}(t_1)} \qquad [7.3]$$

which increases tending towards

$$\underline{\Omega}(N) = \frac{N - n_{explor}(t_1)}{n_{explor}(t_1)} \qquad [7.4]$$

However, in practice, as soon as the budget (the maximum number of samplings) is much smaller than the number of points of the search space, there will still be unexplored subdomains. Hence, as we shall see now, it is for example possible to predefine a profile of constant value or even decreasing value at least as long as the number of sampled points remains much lower than the total number of points of the search space. Otherwise, for example, for explicitly discrete problems of small size, Theorem 7.1 is perfectly suitable and, therefore, does not allow any strategy in terms of exploitation and exploration.

8

The Explo2 Algorithm

Coding exploitation is relatively simple, even when using a D-sphere $S\,(i,\alpha r)$. In fact, it suffices to randomly sample in its interior, in a uniform or non-uniform manner (see source code A.12.1).

With a D-cube, it is even easier to sample randomly in its interior and if this must be done according to a probabilistic distribution denser toward the center, then we can, for example, apply a similar approach to that given for the greedy algorithm (see section A.11): each coordinate of the new point is an instance of the distribution

$$\frac{1}{K}\sum_{k=1}^{K} U\,(0,1) \qquad\qquad [8.1]$$

up to a linear transformation (translation to center in i and homothety to adjust the support to the side of the D-cube). The larger K is, the more closely the distribution approaches the normal distribution.

However, for exploration, it is more complicated. How, indeed, can we sample inside a complexly shaped domain, which is the complementary (with respect to the search space) of a union of D-spheres or D-cubes? In the implementation covered in Chapter 7, it is well understood that when the number of sampled positions (and thereby of potential exploitation domains) increases, this procedure is likely to take longer, before a satisfactory point is found.

Nonetheless, the experiment shows that the number of attempts remains reasonable in general, except in dimension 1, where it is better to use the specific method. It should also be noted that tested positions are not evaluated (it is merely verified that they are in fact exploration positions), and thus, if the budget is precisely a maximum number of evaluations, then it is not affected.

On the contrary, what is *not* reasonable is to use this algorithm for problems of significant dimension, specifically because of the exploration method, which, despite being formally correct, becomes prohibitive in terms of computational time (see Explo2+ for a possible compromise, in section A.10).

Independently of the methods used, to measure the exploitation/ exploration ratio, the number of sampled points has to mainly be counted according to each strategy, and therefrom to accurately achieve the ratio. Let us see what happens with a very simple optimizer written for the occasion.

8.1. The algorithm

Our optimizer samples points in the search space, as either exploitation or exploration trying to follow as closely as possible a balance profile initially provided by the user.

It is not designed to be particularly effective but to highlight the influence of the balance profile. However, it does not prove to be particularly bad in terms of performance. In this regard, the point of view of practitioners should be recalled, engineers for example, who have to use an optimizer within a given budget. Their objective is to obtain the best possible result with this constraint. Hence, for their part, the comparisons of optimizers focusing on averages or medians are not relevant. Nor even, moreover, most comparisons based on the minima that were found, if the probability of achieving them is not given, as is most often.

Indeed, it is hardly helpful to know that, with a given testing problem and with a given budget, optimizer A finds the solution 0.001 and optimizer B only 0.01 when, in the first case, it is in fact with a very low probability. Better, if the probability of the second case is very strong, then engineers might even prefer optimizer B.

Therefore, a comparison should be made using the cumulative distributions of the results on a large enough number of runs of optimizers A and B to be compared. In particular, if their curves intersect, none of the propositions "A is better than B", "B is better than A" and "A and B are equivalent" is correct (see section A.9). In this case, both optimizers are, literally, in-comparable.

At the least, a table should be presented comprising the minimum m found by each optimizer including an estimate of the probability of its occurrence p. For example, if the total budget is B, users can launch the optimizer n times with a partial budget $\frac{B}{n}$ and then they know that it has the probability $1 - (1 - p)^n$ of finding this minimum. It should, however, be noted that this is not necessarily the optimal utilization of a total budget. It may be more appropriate to launch multiple runs with different partial budgets (for more details, see for example, Clerc (2015)).

If the results from a few problems are thus presented to compare Explo2 and APS (which, it should be reminded, exceeds a large number of optimizers with conventional sets of test cases, see Omran and Clerc (2016) and Omran and Clerc (2017), Table 8.1 is obtained. In each case, the budget (as the maximum number of evaluations) is that estimated automatically by APS according to dimension D of the problem, by the formula $B = \left\lfloor 2450\sqrt{D} \right\rfloor$. Details about the problems of the CEC 2011 competition can be found in Das and Suganthan (2011). For Explo2, balance profile 6, explained below in 8.1.1, has been used, and the domains are D-cubes.

Problem	Dimension	Budget	APS		Explo2 profile 6 $\alpha = 0.1$	
			Minimum	Probability	Minimum	Probability
CEC 2011. The Bifunctional Catalyst Blend Optimal Control Problem	1	2,400	1.151489×10^{-5}*	1	1.151489×10^{-5}*	1
Gears (Gear Train)	4	4,900	2.700857×10^{-12}*	0.03	2.700857×10^{-12}*	0.01
Pressure vessel	4	4,900	$6,059.83^{1}$	0.01	7,084.08	0.01
CEC 2011. Transmission Network Expansion Planning (TNEP) Problem	7	6,400	220*	1	220*	0.04

1 The real minimum is 6,059.714335048436. See section A.5.2. To find it at least once in a hundred runs, APS needs a budget of about 10,000 evaluations.

Table 8.1. *Summary comparison, APS versus Explo2. The probability of finding the indicated minimum is estimated over 100 runs. An asterisk indicates that this is actually the global minimum*

As expected Explo2 is not as good as APS[1]. However, it becomes very greedy in terms of computation time when the dimension increases. However, as stated, its purpose here is not effectiveness. It is moreover possible to make it much faster by modifying its exploration technique (see section A.10). It should be noted that it is far from ridiculous, while being rather rudimentary. Here is its pseudocode:

The search space is first normalized in $\{0,1\}^D$. Naturally, any point evaluation is done by reconverting it to the original space. In this version, we do not test if a point has already been sampled. It is therefore not adapted to explicitly discrete problems with small search spaces.

```
Define budget B;
Define the selection parameter α ∈ ]0,1];
Define the desired balance profile Ω on [2, B];
Initialize a point at the center of the search
space
and N₀ − 1 random points;
nbExploit=0; nbExplore=N₀;
Evaluate the N₀ points;
Sort them by order of increasing value;
Note the best value f_min and its position x_min;
N_E = N₀; % Number of evaluations
While N_E < B

    If nbExploit/nbExplore<Ω(N_E) expl=1;
    If nbExploit/nbExplore>Ω(N_E) expl=2;
    If nbExploit/nbExplore=Ω(N_E) expl=1 or 2
    randomly;
    If expl=1
```

1 A mechanism, which partially explains the superiority of APS, as also that of other methods, is the presence of stagnation detection. APS decides "along the way" if it should do exploration or exploitation. No predefined balance profile. On the other hand, as already pointed out, since it "forgets" some positions already evaluated, it can never be guaranteed that its exploration is a real one. And stagnation detection, even probabilistic as in APS, introduces some degree of arbitrariness, in addition to a balance profile.

```
                    Randomly choose the exploitation point x*
                    among the αN₀;
                    Apply an exploitation method of center x*
                    to find the new point x (N_E);
           If expl=2

                    Apply an exploration method
                    (consistent with the exploitation method)
                    to find the new point x (N_E);
           Evaluate f (x (N_E));
           If f (x (N_E)) < f_min
              f (x (N_E)) → f_min
              x (N_E) → x_min
           Re-sort the points;
```

Box 8.1. *Explo2, pseudocode. Search for the minimum of the function f*

Nonetheless, what matters here is not really the intrinsic effectiveness to this optimizer, but the influence of the balance profile on its performance. Let us first choose a problem of average difficulty, for example, the Alpine function.

Defined for any point $x = (x_1, x_2, \ldots, x_D)$ of $[0, 4D]^D$:

$$f(x) = \sum_{d=1}^{D} |(x_d - d) \sin(x_d - d)| + a |x_d - d| \qquad [8.2]$$

The zero global minimum is in $(1, 2, \ldots, D)$. For the figure and the tests, $D = 2$ and $a = 0, 1$.

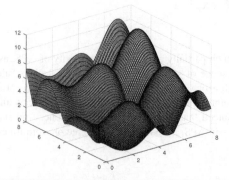

Box 8.2. *Alpine function*

8.1.1. *Influence of the balance profile*

Then, we apply Explo2 to our problem by varying the profile and keeping the other parameters same:

– initial population $N_0 = 90$;

– selection parameter 0.2;

– exploitation method 1 (using D-spheres);

– exploration method 1 (using loop of attempts);

– 100 runs of 1,000 evaluations each.

Table 8.2 presents eight profiles and shows how Explo2 tries to "follow" them during the search process. It should be noted that all these profiles begin with N_0 null values, since it is recognized that the first random samplings are of exploration, although this is not always correct, because it is indeed possible that a point randomly drawn be inside the exploitation domain of another, even if the probability of this example is generally negligible. Hence, some profiles present a discontinuity at the beginning that Explo2 cannot perfectly negotiate (profiles 1, 2 and 8).

For comparing behaviors, we shall apply here the method consisting of plotting the graphs of the cumulative distribution functions (CDF) of the results, over 100 runs (Figure 8.1), used for example in Omran and Clerc (2017).

Profile 6 is clearly the best, closely followed by number 2. It should be noted that these are two profiles that induce few exploitations only (at most half less than explorations). On the contrary, profile 5 is apparently the worst, probably due to the fact that, for its part, it induces too many exploitations (up to 1.5 times more than exploration). Nonetheless, if a user demanding very good results (less than 10^{-3}) would not be able to make a decision between the latter and number 8, then the latter would be the best of both, as shown in the figure enlargement.

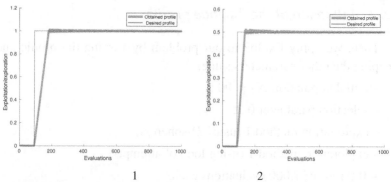

1   2

No.	Description of the desired profile (the interval $[2, N_0]$ is omitted, where the profile is null).
1	Constant, equal to 1. This profile means perfect balance at any moment between exploitation and exploration.
2	Constant, equal to $\omega < 1$. There must therefore be at any moment $\frac{1}{\omega}$ times more exploration points than exploitation points.

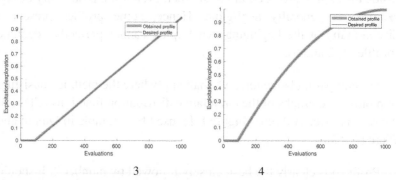

3   4

No.	Description of the desired profile (the interval $[2, N_0]$ is omitted, where the profile is null).
3	Linear-increasing towards balance (final value 1). Constantly less exploitation than exploration with a tendency towards perfect balance.
4	Inverse parabolic increasing towards balance (final value 1). Constantly less exploitation than exploration, but yet still more than the previous case and still with a tendency to perfect balance.

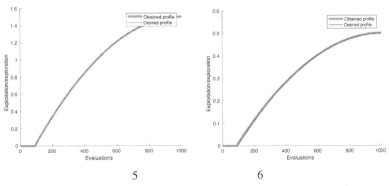

	5	6

No.	Description of the desired profile (the interval $[2, N_0]$ is omitted, where the profile is null).
5	Inverse parabolic increasing, to a value greater than 1. From a given time, the total number of exploitations exceeds that of explorations.
6	Inverse parabolic increasing, towards a value smaller than 1. At any time, the total number of explorations exceeds that of exploitations.

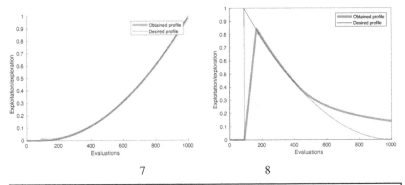

	7	8

No.	Description of the desired profile (the interval $[2, N_0]$ is omitted, where the profile is null).
7	Parabolic increasing towards 1. Constantly less exploitations than explorations, as in profile 6, but more significantly pronounced, and with a tendency towards perfect balance.
8	Linearly decreasing. First essentially exploitation, then mainly exploration. Tendency to pure exploration.

Table 8.2. *A few typical profiles. The figures are for 1,000 evaluations, the budget used here in the tests, but similar profiles are possible for any other budget*

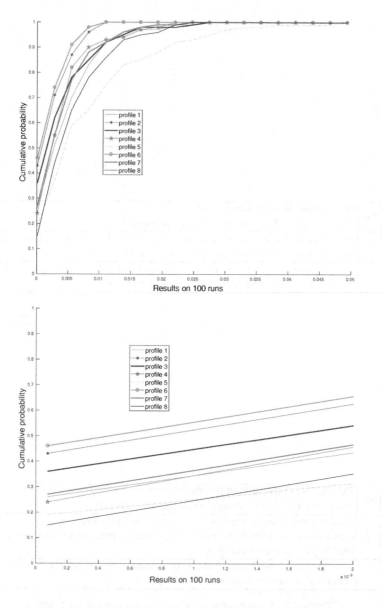

Figure 8.1. *Alpine function, profiles 1 to 8 for a budget of 1,000 evaluations. Cumulative distributions of the results. The bottom figure is an enlargement showing that for result values smaller than 10^{-3}, profile 5 surpasses profile 8, despite the fact that it remains significantly worse than all the others*

Contrary to what suggests the expression often encountered "It is important to balance exploitation and exploration", it can be seen that the profiles that tend to achieve this balance are not the best choices.

The curves that intersect, such as numbers 3 and 7, cannot be globally interpreted. If the user had to choose between both and would absolutely require a result smaller than 0.005, even with low probability, then profile 3 would be preferable. However, if a higher probability is preferred considering a higher result, then profile 7 is the winner.

And curves that cross one another several times, such as numbers 4 and 7, require more detailed interpretations.

One might think that the relative efficiencies of the profiles are independent of the maximum budget (the maximum admissible search effort). In fact, this assumption is often inaccurate, especially for problems of low modality, because a balance profile can be seen as a strategic guide.

However, if only a small budget is available, then it is not unreasonable to adopt a risky strategy achieving less explorations and faster starting exploitations around positions *a priori* interesting and, as a result, the most effective profiles are not necessarily the same ones.

For our Alpine problem, let us consider, for example, profiles 6 and 8, taking a budget of only 200 evaluations (see Figure 8.2).

We then obtain the cumulated probabilities in Figure 8.3. It can now be seen that, conversely to the previous situation, profile 8 gives better results than profile 6.

Moreover, we have something similar with the PSO versions for which the coefficient of inertia is linearly decreasing according to the number of evaluations with respect to the maximum number of evaluations allowed. The smaller the latter, the faster the decrease and, therefore, the more it focuses on short displacements around promising positions, at the expense of displacements of larger scale (analogous to explorations). And for some problems, especially those of low modality, this may be more effective than performing "too many" explorations.

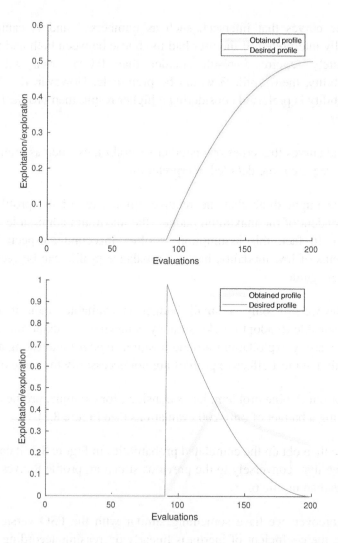

Figure 8.2. *Profiles 6 and 8 for a budget of 200 evaluations. For a color version of this image, see www.iste.co.uk/clerc/iterative.zip*

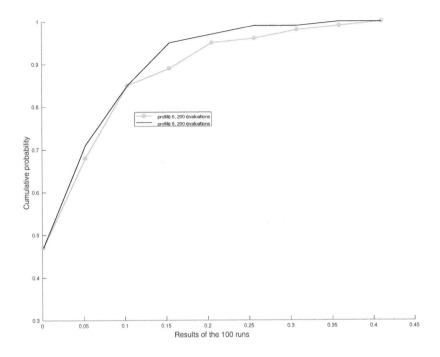

Figure 8.3. *Alpine function, profiles 6 and 8, for a budget of 200 evaluations. Cumulative probability of the results. For a color version of this image, see www.iste.co.uk/clerc/iterative.zip*

8.2. Subjective numerical summary of a distribution of results

Comparisons of CDFs are objective criteria, but as seen, they can lead to undecidable situations or, at least, be difficult to interpret when curves intersect. On the contrary, if introducing subjectivity in the form of a curve of user-defined quality for the different results obtained, we can then represent each CDF using a single numeric value, which allows a total ordering relation. The downside, obviously, is that this method "imposes" a classification depending on the quality curve. Let us observe this using examples.

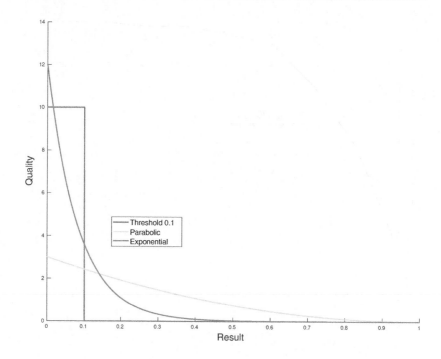

Figure 8.4. *Some quality curves, normalized on [0,1]. For a color version of this image, see www.iste.co.uk/clerc/iterative.zip*

Figure 8.4 presents three curves of typical quality:

– with threshold. Users only accept results below a certain threshold and then assign to each one the same value. This is the curve implicitly utilized when one refers to success rates;

– parabolic decreasing. Users prefer best results (smaller ones), but allow poorer results;

– exponential decreasing. Users assign a high value to very good results alone. The value given to others is never quite zero, but quickly becomes negligible.

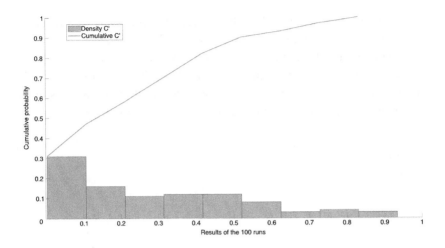

Figure 8.5. *Example of cumulative distribution and of the associated probability density (estimated over 10 classes)*

Let C be a cumulative distribution defined on results $[a, b]$ and C' its associated probability density. Let Q be a normalized quality curve defined in $[0, 1]$. The subjective numerical value given by the user to distribution C is given by

$$v_P(C) = \int_{r=a}^{b} C'(x) Q\left(\frac{r-a}{b-a}\right) dx \qquad [8.3]$$

The interpretation is that, via the curve Q, users allocate a "weight" to each result r and the integral above accumulates these weights. It should be noted that in practice C' is calculated using finite differences such as $\frac{C(r_{i+1})-C(r_i)}{r_{i+1}-r_i}$, where r_i is the result of the i-th optimizer run and the integral itself is actually a finite sum. This implies that to have correct estimates, quite a large number of runs are necessary, typically at least 100.

Let us apply this method to the results given by Explo2 with the Alpine function. Every time a given balance profile is used, the pair (algorithm, profile) can be considered to be a particular optimizer. For the eight profiles seen earlier, the different representative values of Table 8.3 can be obtained according to the chosen quality curve. The associated figure shows that the three quality curves do not exactly give the same classification for our eight optimizers. The best two (6 and 2) are the same, but for example, the worst one is different, as a result of the intersection of the distribution curves visible in Figure 8.1.

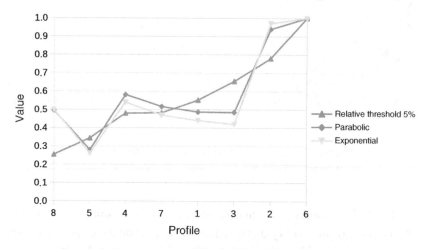

Profile	Relative threshold 5%	Parabolic	Exponential
8	0.254	0.494	0.499
5	0.343	0.278	0.260
4	0.479	0.581	0.540
7	0.481	0.516	0.469
1	0.552	0.486	0.440
3	0.655	0.484	0.420
2	0.779	0.939	0.971
6	1.000	1.000	1.000

Table 8.3. *Alpine function, profiles 1 to 8 for a budget of 1,000 evaluations. Representative values of the distributions of results, according to the three quality curves of Figure 8.4. The relative threshold is given as a percentage of the span of the results. In each column, the values have been normalized (maximum 1). The classification is done with respect to the first curve (relative threshold of 5%)*

In fact, it could even be easily shown that using another profile with threshold would still change the classification. This type of profile is not robust and hence it is best to carefully consider any comparison of optimizers achieved using success rates, especially if, this comparison is made without taking into account the underlying probability distribution[2].

---

2 Two success rates are significantly different with a probability of 95% only if their difference is greater than $\frac{3}{\text{no. of tests}}$ (see Eric D. Taillard (2003)).

9

Balance and Perceived Difficulty

To study the relationships between balance profiles and the perceived difficulty of a problem for a given optimizer, we simplify as much as possible:

– by considering constant profiles of different values h, denoted as $\underline{\Omega}_h$;

– by defining pair-based optimizers (Explo2 algorithm, profile), which we shall denote here by $\text{Explo2}(\underline{\Omega}_h)$;

– by starting from the smallest possible initial population (2, with Explo2).

9.1. Constant profile-based experiments

Let us revisit our little Alpine problem in dimension 2 and execute $\text{Explo2}(\underline{\Omega}_h)$ a hundred times for values of h increasing from 0.2 to 1.5 and a budget of 200 evaluations for each run. Figure 9.1 shows with an example ($h = 0.4$) how the optimizer quickly "catches" the desired profile.

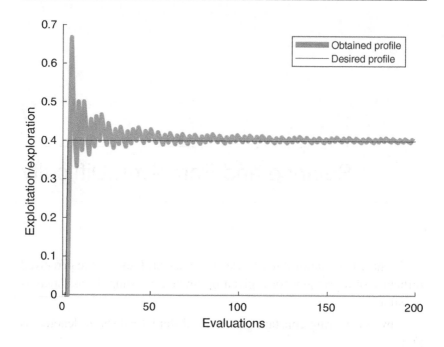

Figure 9.1. *A constant profile and the
actual profile generated by Explo2*

The CDFs obtained (actually, a magnified view of the results smaller than 0.04) are shown in Figure 9.2. With such a bare example, it can clearly be observed that it is more beneficial to do more explorations than exploitations. The profile of value 1 (perfect balance) gives only a mediocre optimizer. When one requires more exploitations than explorations ($h > 1$), effectiveness continues to deteriorate.

Naturally, with more sophisticated algorithms, conclusions would not be as clear-cut, due to the influence of other mechanisms. However, the experiment shows that the following small rule proves to be useful.

CLAIM 9.1.– Always keeping the exploitation/exploration ratio significantly smaller than 1 improves effectiveness.

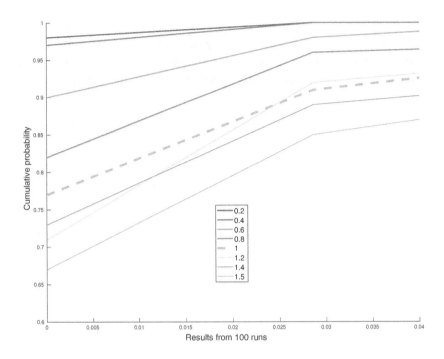

Figure 9.2. *Distributions of the results of the Explo2($\underline{\Omega}_h$) optimizers for different values of h and with the 2D Alpine problem. It is preferable to significantly achieve fewer exploitations than explorations. For a color version of this image, see www.iste.co.uk/clerc/iterative.zip*

9.2. Calculated difficulty vs perceived difficulty

We have defined difficulty measures, in particular $\delta^*_{\neg NisB}$, which does not need to know the landscape structure, and δ_0, which takes this structure into account. However, as already pointed out, this information is rarely available for problems that have not specifically been created so that it would be available.

Furthermore, we have defined the perceived difficulty (section 2.8) by an optimizer, which depends on the user's preferences for the threshold of acceptability of the result and its associated probability.

It is then possible to define a series of problems whose estimated difficulties $\delta^*_{\neg NisB}$ increase in a significantly different fashion from perceived difficulties. This is, for example, the case with certain scalable problems defined by a formula, where the dimension is a parameter.

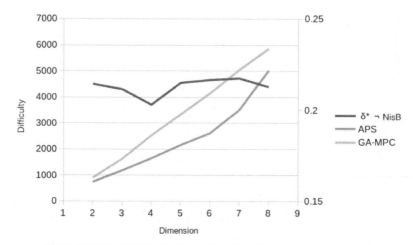

Dimension	$\delta^*_{\neg NisB}$	Perceived difficulty		
		APS	MVMO-SH	GA-MPC
1	0.1206	184	Rate of 80% inaccessible. Maximum 78%	270
2	0.2142	736		900
3	0.2114	1178		1620
4	0.2029	1644		2520
5	0.2149	2152		3330
6	0.2165	2604		4140
7	0.2174	3503		5040
8	0.2127	5015		5850

Table 9.1. *Estimated and perceived difficulties for the Alpine problem according to the dimension. Here, the perceived difficulty is the number of evaluations necessary to find a solution of value less than 0.001 with a probability of at least 80%. For the three optimizers, the population is 90. GA-MPC always terminates a complete iteration, hence multiple values of population effort. Beyond dimension 1, the estimated difficulty $\delta^*_{\neg NisB}$ is practically constant, whereas the perceived difficulties significantly increase*

However, the important thing is the tendency. In general, there is consistency (see section 2.7.2), but no relationship between the ratios of values. Indeed, it should be recalled that calculated measures only enable a classification of a set of problems and, moreover, only for optimizers that explicitly or implicitly assume that "nearer is better", even if this concerns almost all of them. Therefore, one should be careful not to believe that a small difference in the measures calculated implies a small difference between the necessary search efforts.

In addition, there are exceptions, especially with $\delta^*_{\neg NisB}$. Thereby, in Table 9.1 for the Alpine function (section 8.1), the difficulty $\delta^*_{\neg NisB}$ is almost constant[1] while perceived difficulties (search efforts) significantly increase. This justifies the approach consisting of building known structure landscapes in order to utilize a measure that takes them into account, for example, δ_0 or others that are more sophisticated and that remain to be defined.

---

1 The number of local basins increases, but their size decreases in a sufficiently uniform manner that the two effects offset each other.

Appendix

A.1. Pigeonhole principle and monotonicity

In its simple form, this can thus be stated as:

CLAIM A.1.– If n objects are placed in m boxes and $n > m$, then at least one box contains several objects.

Currently (June 2018), the oldest known application is in the book by Jean Leurechon in 1622 (Lereuchon 1692), regarding the fact that there necessarily exist two women who have the same number of hairs.

Here, if we define $I_N = \left\{0, \frac{1}{N-1}, \frac{2}{N-1}, \ldots, 1\right\}$, then this principle provides a possible demonstration to the following small theorem:

THEOREM A.1.– *There are only two strictly monotonic maps I_N in I_N: $f_1(x) = x$ and $f_2(x) = 1 - x$.*

It is obvious that these two maps are strictly monotonic. We assume that there exists another one g, increasing for example. We assume the strict inclusion $g(I_N) \subset I_N$. Let $m = |g(I_N)|$. This is the number of "boxes". Since we have $|I_N| = N > m$, at least one box contains two elements of $g(I_N)$. In other words, at least two or more elements x_1 and x_2 of I_N have the same value by g and monotonicity cannot be strict. One must therefore have $g(I_N) = I_N$ and g can be seen as performing a permutation of the elements of I_N. However, the only permutation preserving the order of the elements is the identity, and therefore, $g = f_1$. A similar reasoning would show that if g is decreasing, then $g = f_2$.

REMARK A.1.– It can be specified that if there were pairs such as $g(x_1) = g(x_2)$, then for at least one of these, the two elements would be adjacent and would thus form a plateau. Indeed, otherwise, there would be x_3 such that $x_1 < x_3 < x_2$ with $g(x_1) < g(x_3) < g(x_2)$, which is impossible.

A.2. Similarities between optimizers

Despite their differences, the optimizers used as examples in this book have in fact great similarities. For more details, see the references already given: APS (Omran and Clerc 2017), MVMO-SH (MVMO), GA-MPC (Elsayed *et al.* 2011) and SAMODE (Elsayed *et al.* 2011).

We saw in section 2.7.2 on consistencies that for these optimizers, perceived difficulties of problems can be classified in the same order. This is an intriguing fact at first glance because if we consider the informal descriptions of these algorithms, then they make use of rather different mechanisms.

However, if one examines in detail the pseudo-codes or, better, the source codes, which are ultimately the only real tools producing the results presented, then great similarities can be found in reality, which can be summarized as follows:

– they manipulate a population, whether it is called agents, individuals, positions or other. Let us here refer thereto as "positions";

– they start with a phase of random initialization of the positions, according to the uniform distribution;

– in the case of stagnation (but here detection criteria can be different), some positions are randomly displaced;

– and, especially, the most crucial point is that they all explicitly or implicitly assume that for the landscape under study, the property "nearer is better" (NisB) is true in probability (see the notion of reliable function in section 3.1).

The last point implies that if the property does not hold, that is, if the landscape is that of a deceptive function, then these algorithms will be ineffective. And as such, this suggests two things:

– that it is possible to design an optimizer that does not make this assumption and that is effective with deceptive functions but ineffective with reliable functions;

– that if there is a detection mechanism available, at least probabilistic, of the nature of the function (reliable or deceptive), then this optimizer can be hybridized with a more conventional one, such as the four that we have seen. The resulting algorithm should then be effective in all the cases.

A.3. Optimizer signature

This characteristic element is presented in detail in Clerc (2015). Let us just present a summary here.

Using the function Plateau, defined on $[-1, 1]^2$ by $f(x_1, x_2) = 1$, imposes on us to search for a null minimum, which is impossible. Then, the set of sampled positions brings forward a number of optimizer biases, the main ones being centrality bias and the boundary bias.

Typically, 10 runs of 1,000 evaluations are achieved and "signatures" are obtained such as those of the figure, for various parameterizations of APS (Figure A.1).

In general, centrality bias is all the more pronounced when the optimizer proceeds randomly. Naturally, this bias implies an overestimation of effectiveness if the test set includes landscapes whose optimum is precisely at the center of the search space or even simply close to it.

A.4. Non-NisB difficulties of a unimodal function

In simple cases, we can exactly calculate the two measures $\delta_{\neg NisB}$ and $\delta^*_{\neg NisB}$, instead of estimating them using a Monte Carlo method. For example, consider the parabola $f(x) = (x - a)^2$, with $0 \leq a \leq 1$.

In fact, incidentally, the calculations here below are valid for every unimodal function of minimum at a, which can be seen as the translated form of a symmetric function. For example, $(x - a)^{2k}$, or $1 - \sin(\pi(x - a))$.

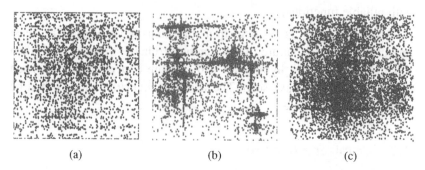

(a)   (b)   (c)

Figure A.1. *A few APS signatures. (a) Population of 40, disk-based local search. 6.8% of the points on the boundary. Slight centrality bias. (b) Population of 12, rectangle-based local search. 1.6% of the points on the boundary. Exploitation bias particularly clear around the ten initial positions, accompanied by axial bias for each planar direction. (c) Population of 40, rectangle-based local search. 5.5% of the points on the boundary. Exploitation biases merge into some kind of offset centrality bias*

A.4.1. $\delta_{\neg NisB}$ *measure*

All position triplets are taken into account. Neutral triplets being negligible, we simply have to calculate the measure of the set of W-type triplets:

By symmetry, we can only study the case $a \leq \frac{1}{2}$. If, in a triplet $\{x_1, x_2, x_3\}$, the x_i are all smaller or all larger than a, then the triplet is necessarily of type B. In the particular case $a = \frac{1}{2}$, and due to the fact that $f(x_1) \leq f(x_2) \leq f(x_3)$, we have, for W-type triplets

$$
\mu(W) = \int_{x_1=0}^{1} \int_{x_2=x_1}^{1} \int_{x3=x2}^{1} dx_3 dx_2 dx_3 = \frac{1}{6} \qquad \text{[A.1]}
$$

If $a < \frac{1}{2}$, then W is formed of two subsets: W_1, whose triplets are such that the three x_i are in $[0, a]$, and W_2 containing all the other triplets. Analogously to the case $a = \frac{1}{2}$, it yields that

$$\mu\left(W_1\right) = \frac{1}{6}\left(\frac{a}{\frac{1}{2}}\right)^3 = \frac{4}{3}a^3 \qquad\qquad \text{[A.2]}$$

For W_2, scenarios are constrained by a set of conditions:

$$\begin{aligned} &x_1 \in \,]a, 2a] \\ &x_2 \in [\max\left(0, 2a - x_1\right),] \\ &x_3 \in \,]2a - x_2, \min\left(2x_1 - x_2, 1\right)] \end{aligned} \qquad\qquad \text{[A.3]}$$

They define a polyhedron in I^3 whose vertices are (see Figure A.2)

$$\begin{aligned} v_1 &= (a, 0, 0) \\ v_2 &= (2a, 0, 0) \\ v_3 &= \left(\frac{4a}{3}, \frac{2a}{3}, 0\right) \\ v_4 &= \left(\min\left(\frac{1}{2}, 2a\right), 0, \min\left(1 - 2a, 1\right)\right) \\ v_5 &= (2a, 0, \min\left(1 - 2a, 1\right)) \\ v_6 &= \left(\min\left(\frac{2a+1}{3}, 2a\right), \max\left(0, \frac{4a-1}{3}\right), \min\left(1 - 2a, 1\right)\right) \end{aligned} \qquad\qquad \text{[A.4]}$$

Let V be its volume. To calculate the measure μ of the set of corresponding triplets, we merely multiply it by the ratio between the volume of I^3, that is, 1, and that of A, the set of all triplets, which is $\lim\limits_{N \to \infty} \frac{6N^3}{N(N-1)(N-2)} = 6$.

In the case $a \leq \frac{1}{4}$, the vertices v_4, v_5 and v_6 are overlapping. Then, to calculate V, the two subcases $a \in \left[0, \frac{1}{4}\right]$ and $a \in \left]\frac{1}{4}, 1\right]$ can be considered. In the first, the polyhedron is a pyramid with a triangular base, which easily gives $\mu\left(W_2\right) = \frac{4}{3}a^3$, and thus

$$\mu\left(W\right) = \frac{8}{3}a^3 \qquad\qquad \text{[A.5]}$$

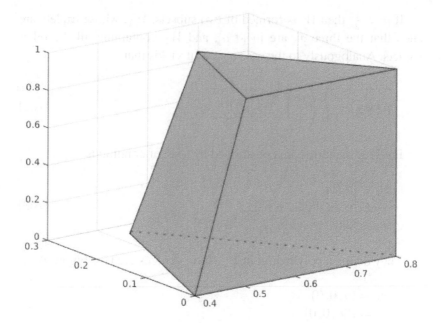

Figure A.2. *The polyhedron defining W_2, for $a = 0.4$*

In the second, the polyhedron is slightly more complicated, but it can be seen as the intersection of two pyramids and, ultimately, its volume is $V = -\frac{14}{9}a^3 + \frac{4}{3}a^2 - \frac{a}{3} + \frac{1}{36}$, from which

$$\mu\left(W\right) = -8a^3 + 8a^2 - 2a + \frac{1}{6} \qquad\qquad [A.6]$$

Figure A.3 represents this measure for values of a $\left[0, \frac{1}{2}\right]$. For values in $\left]\frac{1}{2}, 1\right]$, the measure can be inferred by symmetry. We then have the following theorem.

THEOREM A.2.– *The non-NisB difficulty $(\delta_{\neg NisB})$ of the parabola $f\left(x\right) = \left(x - a\right)^2$ on $[0, 1]$ is at most equal to $\frac{1}{6}$, for $a = \frac{1}{2}$.*

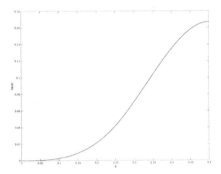

Figure A.3. *Non-NisB difficulty of the parabola* $(x - a)^2$, *for* $a \in \left[0, \frac{1}{2}\right]$. *For* $a > \frac{1}{2}$, *we have the symmetrical curve decreasing to zero.*

A.4.2. *Measure* $\delta^*_{\neg NisB}$

The calculation is similar but much easier because now only the triplets $\{a, x_2, x_3\}$ are being considered, since a is the position of the minimum. We have $f(a) < f(x_2) < f(x_3)$. The only disjoint cases defining W are now:

$$\begin{cases} x_3 < a < x_2 \\ a - x_3 > x_2 - a \end{cases}$$

and its symmetrical, from which

$$\mu(W) = 2 \int\limits_{x_3=0}^{a} \int\limits_{x_2=2a-x_3}^{y} dx_3 dx_2 \qquad \text{[A.7]}$$

with $f(y) = f(x_3)$. As a result thereof, if the curve is symmetrical around a, as the parabola studied above, then $y = 2a - x_3$ and the measure $\mu(W)$ is zero. If the curve is not symmetrical, the measure varies according to the significance of the asymmetry. For example, with the curve of Figure A.4, it can easily be found that

$$\mu(W) = a - 2a^2 \qquad \text{[A.8]}$$

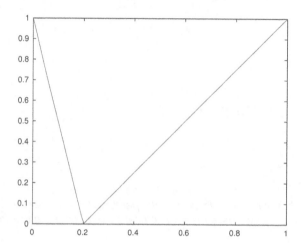

Figure A.4. *Unimodal function composed of two linear ones*

A.5. A few test functions

Here, we will not provide again details of test cases CEC 2005 and CEC 2011, which can be found in Suganthan *et al.* (2005) and Das and Suganthan (2011), but mainly the description of two small problems used for the algorithm Explo2 (see Chapter 8).

A.5.1. *Gear train*

The function whose minimum is searched for is given by:

$$f(x) = \left(\frac{1}{\alpha} - \frac{x_1 x_2}{x_3 x_4} \right)^2 \qquad\qquad\qquad [A.9]$$

The search space is $\{12, 13, \ldots, 60\}^4$. Different variations can be obtained by modifying the parameter α. In Sandgren (1990) and Onwubolu and Babu (2004), its value is 6.931. The problem is non-separable multimodal. Given that variables x_1, x_2, on the one hand, and x_3, x_4, on the other hand, play the same role, there are several solutions. For example, $(16; 19; 43; 49)$ which yields the minimum 2.700857×10^{-12}.

A.5.2. *Pressure vessel*

This problem is presented and discussed in detail in Sandgren (1990), Clerc (2005), and Onwubolu and Babu (2004). It is described by means of four variables:

$$x_1 \in [0.0625; 99] \text{ of granularity } 0.0625$$
$$x_2 \in [0.0625; 99] \text{ of granularity } 0.0625$$
$$x_3 \in]10; 200]$$
$$x_4 \in]10; 200]$$

and three constraints:

$$g_1 := 0.0193x_3 - x_1 \leq 0$$
$$g_2 := 0.00954x_3 - x_2 \leq 0$$
$$g_3 := 750 \times 1728 - \pi x_3^2 \left(x_4 + \tfrac{4}{3}x_3\right) \leq 0$$

The function f is defined by:

$$f\left(x_1 x_2, x_3, x_4\right) = 0.06224 x_1 x_3 x_4 + 1.7781 x_2 x_3^2$$
$$+ x_1^2 \left(3.1661x + 19,84x_3\right)$$

The problem is multimodal, non-separable. Analytically, the minimum is at the point $x^* = (0.8125; 0.4375; 42.0984455958549;$ $176.6365958424394)$ with $f(x^*) = 6059.714335048436$ (Yang *et al.* 2013).

A.6. Equivalent functions

In the analysis, the notion of equivalency of two functions f and g is local (equal behavior in the neighborhood of a point). However, from the optimization point of view, it can be extended. Suppose that we have two bijections φ_X and φ_V of I in I, with the following properties:

  $- \varphi_X$ is continuous[1], strictly monotonic, $\varphi_X(0) = 0$, $\varphi_X(1) = 1$;

---

1 Any interval of I contains an infinite number of points and a notion of continuity can be defined similar to that on real numbers $\mathbb{R}$.

– φ_V is continuous strictly increasing. This implies that φ_V^{-1} is also strictly increasing.

Thus, the formal definition of the *optim-equivalence* is

$$f \sim g \iff \forall x \in I, \varphi_V\left(g\left(x\right)\right) = f\left(\varphi_X\left(x\right)\right)$$

which can be rewritten less symmetrically as

$$f \sim g \iff \forall x \in I, g\left(x\right) = \varphi_V^{-1}\left(f\left(\varphi_X\left(x\right)\right)\right)$$

An intuitive interpretation is that g is built by "deforming" f on the definition space and also on the space of values, while respecting the ordering relation between the values of f. For example, the two functions of Figure A.5 are optim-equivalent, with $\varphi_X\left(x\right) = x^2$ and $\varphi_V^{-1}\left(v\right) = 0.2 + 0.7\sqrt{v}$, and every unimodal function is also optim-equivalent.

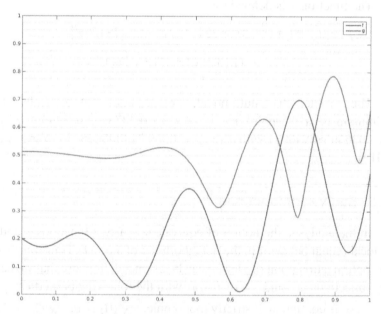

Figure A.5. *Two optim-equivalent functions. The relative positions and the relative values of optima are the same. For a color version of this image, see www.iste.co.uk/clerc/iterative.zip*

An iterative optimizer that takes into account the ranks of the values of the function and not these values themselves – such as, for example, a classical particle swarm optimizer – will generate two sequences of points sampled as images of one another by φ_X or φ_X^{-1}, provided of course that the random number generator being used is initialized in the same way.

Two optim-equivalent landscapes share the same structure at level 1 (same number of basins and same number of plateaus) but nothing else.

A.7. Examples of deceptive functions

Description files of the functions of Table A.1 are given in section A.13. For landscapes T_3 and T_5, the local minimum is at 0.01, but its value is 0.01 for T_5 and 0.001 for T_3, which makes this last problem very difficult.

Readers who are skeptical as to the difficulty of these problems or simply curious could try to address them with their favorite optimizer. Let us recall the rules of the game: for an acceptability threshold (admissible error) of 0.0001, estimate the average effort (such as the number of evaluations) which gives a success rate of 80%.

Figure A.6 shows that the ordering relation given by the measure of difficulty δ_0 is consistent with the one resulting from the average effort for the optimizer APS(6). Nonetheless, the same does not happen here for the measure $\delta_{\neg NisB}$, based on the set of all position triplets, and only approximately for the measure $\delta_{\neg NisB}^*$, which only considers triplets containing the position of the global minimum.

Therefore, when these measures give values higher than 0.5, they may no longer allow correct forecasting as to the gradation of practical difficulties with a given test case.

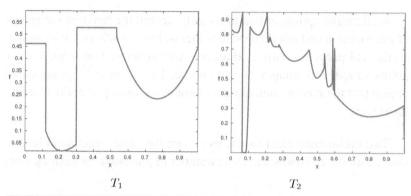

$$T_1 \qquad\qquad\qquad\qquad T_2$$

Text file code	Difficulty $\delta_{\neg NisB}$ (all triplets)	Difficulty $\delta^*_{\neg NisB}$ (triplets (x^*, x_2, x_3))	Difficulty δ_0	Average effort for APS
T_1	0.56	0.50	0.75	89.2
T_2	0.52	0.82	0.84	202.6

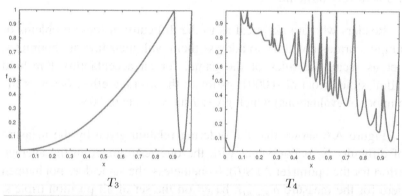

$$T_3 \qquad\qquad\qquad\qquad T_4$$

Text file code	Difficulty $\delta_{\neg NisB}$ (all triplets)	Difficulty $\delta^*_{\neg NisB}$ (triplets (x^*, x_2, x_3))	Difficulty δ_0	Average effort for APS
T_3	0.54	0.86	0.97	>1000
T_4	0.57	0.84	0.79	131.2

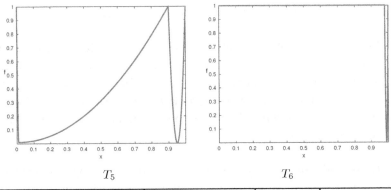

T_5 T_6

Text file code	Difficulty $\delta_{\neg NisB}$ (all triplets)	Difficulty $\delta^*_{\neg NisB}$ (triplets (x^*, x_2, x_3))	Difficulty δ_0	Average effort for APS
T_5	0.54	0.86	0.91	608
T_6	0.999	0.96	0.88	233.8

Table A.1. *A few deceptive functions. The difficulty is increased by plateaus (see T_1 and T_6), but still more probably by spurring decreases that move away from the global minimum*

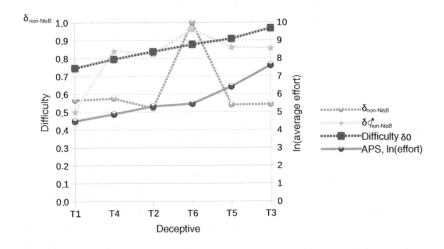

Figure A.6. *Deceptive functions. Difficulty δ_0 and (in logarithmic scale) average effort for APS(6). For a color version of this image, see www.iste.co.uk/clerc/iterative.zip*

A.8. Empirical rules for a measure of difficulty

In this section, I present some of the experiments for evaluating the difficulty of a landscape based on its structure. In this small sample, landscapes are only of dimension 1, to facilitate the representation. Their global minimum has value zero. For all the experiments, 0.001 is given as the *acceptability threshold*, more specifically as the maximal value of an acceptable solution.

Each landscape is supposed to have been created by LandGener[2]. The search space is therefore partitioned into domains that are D-triangles and each domain supports either a plateau or a basin.

The idea is to identify rules that tell us to what extent each domain contributes to global difficulty. These rules may seem obvious, but they are still required to be experimentally validated.

An important point is precisely their domain of validity. On the one hand, they assume that the landscape has only a single global minimum and that the smallest local minimum value remains above the threshold of acceptability. It is obvious that otherwise the difficulty is less. On the other hand, they *a priori* only concern optimizers with the following characteristics:

– iterative;

– stochastic;

– assuming (explicitly or implicitly) that the property "nearer is better" (NisB) is true for the landscape under consideration.

This last point is the most important. Ultimately, a deterministic algorithm can be seen as being stochastic with a random number generator whose distribution function is just a Dirac on value 1. Similarly, a singulative algorithm is just an iterative one with a single step. Moreover, there is, for example, no difference between successively and independently sampling N positions and sampling them once in parallel.

---

2 In fact, they are so simple that I generally directly wrote text files describing them.

In the end, the class of algorithms under consideration is extremely broad. For the experiments described below, I have used several ones that qualitatively give the same results about the evolution of difficulty based on the following criteria:

– the size of the basin of attraction of the global minimum;

– the sizes, values and positions of plateaus;

– the sizes and positions of the basins of attraction of local minima as well as the values of these minima.

In fact, "position" should rather be understood as "the distance to the position of the global minimum" and "value" as "the deviation with respect to the value of global minimal". Furthermore, in short, I shall sometimes use the ellipses *local/global basin* instead of *local/global minimum basin*.

A.8.1. *The contribution of basins*

Let us look into experimental results conducted with the APS algorithm (APS; Omran and Clerc 2017). The Matlab® code of version 12 is freely available. For the purposes of this case, I have slightly modified it, essentially intended the size N of the population. As a matter of fact, originally, APS is rather concerning for rather large problems of dimension D and automatically calculates a size according to the formula

$$N = \left\lfloor 90 \left(1 + \frac{\ln(D)}{250} \right) \right\rfloor \qquad \text{[A.10]}$$

which yields a result always equal to at least 90. For simple landscapes of dimension 1 or 2 that we shall see, this is too much: the search space is "saturated" as early as the initialization and success rates almost always equal to 100%, which does not allow us to clearly see the influence of the different structures.

Moreover, APS works with triplets of individuals. As it is coded, it needs at least two of them and, therefore, a population size of at least six. Therefore, I have imposed $N = 6$ for the small illustrative landscapes that we are going to examine, achieved with the LandGener program (see Chapter 4).

CLAIM A.2.– The difficulty is a decreasing function of the size of the basin of the global minimum.

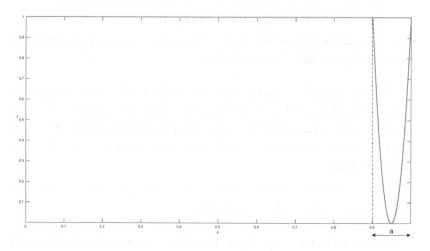

Figure A.7. *A plateau and a global basin of variable size a. For a color version of this image, see www.iste.co.uk/clerc/iterative.zip*

Consider a series of landscapes such as Figure A.7 by varying the size a of the basin. For each basin size, we are then looking for the average effort required to have a success rate of at least 50% on 100 executions, which gives Figure A.8, compatible with the above assertion. In this case, as shown in the model curve, one can even be more specific and say that the formula giving the effort E is of the type

$$E = N + \frac{\alpha_a}{a^{\beta_a}} \qquad [\text{A.11}]$$

with, here, $N = 6$, $\alpha_a = 1.770$ and $\beta_a = 0.209$. Naturally, these values differ depending on the algorithm being used, but it is interesting to note that the overall shape of the curve of decrease is the same for all those that I could test. Qualitatively, this behavior can be understood observing that the first samples are taken randomly and that at least several of them are necessary in the global basin so that the optimizer can then effectively progress.

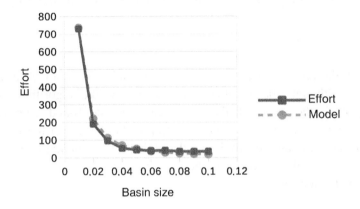

Figure A.8. *Effort versus size of the overall basin. Acceptable solution threshold: 0.001. Desired success rate: at least 50%*

CLAIM A.3.– The contribution to the difficulty of a local minimum is a decreasing function of its value, as long as it lies above the threshold of acceptability.

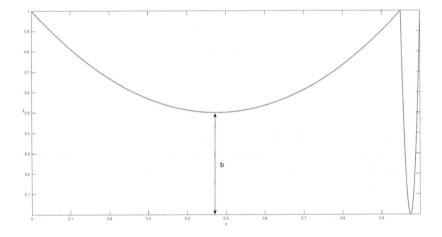

Figure A.9. *Two basins. We vary the value b of the local minimum*

To test this claim, we consider a series of landscapes such as Figure A.10, where only the value b of the local minimum is modified. Figure A.10 is then obtained. Again, the curve can be modeled by

$$E = N + \frac{\alpha_b}{b^{\beta_b}}$$

but, in the present case, with $\alpha_b = 44.67$ and $\beta_b = 0.39$. And, once again, although these values are specific to the algorithm being employed, the trend of the curve can also be found with other optimizers. The qualitative interpretation is that the closer the value of the local minimum gets to that of the global minimum, the more "time is wasted" by the optimizer in the local basin before focusing its effort in the global basin.

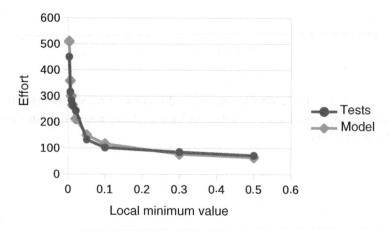

Figure A.10. *Effort versus local minimum value*

Naturally, as pointed out by the end of the claim, this is no longer valid if the value of the local minimum is less than the threshold of acceptability: in this case, on the contrary, the contribution of the local basin reduces the difficulty.

CLAIM A.4.– The contribution to the difficulty of a local minimum varies little according to its distance to the global minimum.

This behavior is slightly less intuitive than the previous ones. In fact, two mechanisms are competing:

– as the local minimum is further away from the global minimum, the optimizer will have more difficulties in sampling inside the basin of the latter;

– as the local minimum is further away from the global minimum, the optimizer will less tend to return to its basin, once it has found at least a few points in the global basin.

To show the influence of these two mechanisms, a set of landscapes is used such as that of Figure A.11. The experiment shows that there is more or less compensation, as can be seen in Figure A.12, although there is a distance for which the contribution to the difficulty is slightly maximal.

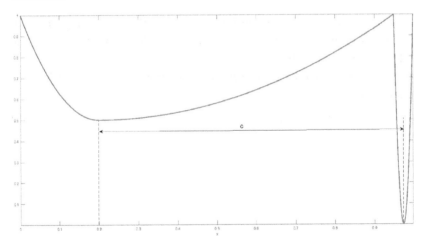

Figure A.11. *Two basins. Position c of the local minimum varies*

CLAIM A.5.– The contribution to the difficulty of a local minimum is an increasing function of the size of its basin.

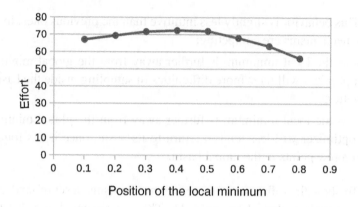

Figure A.12. *Effort versus distance between local minimum and global minimum*

The tests are carried out with landscapes of the type of Figure A.13. The result is given in Figure A.14. Here again, the interpretation is quite intuitive: the larger the local basin, the more difficult it will be for the optimizer to escape thereof. Actually, this property is more or less the dual of claim A.2.

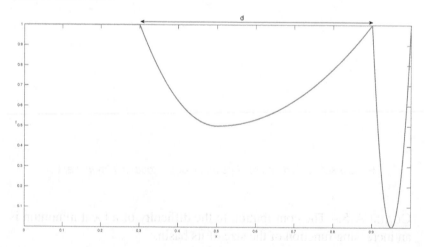

Figure A.13. *Local basin of variable size* d

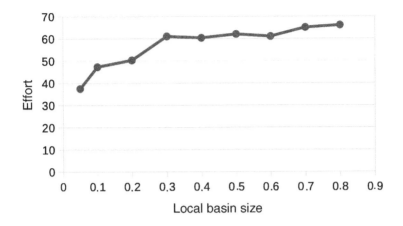

Figure A.14. *Effort versus local basin size*

A.8.2. *The contribution of plateaus*

CLAIM A.6.– The difficulty is an increasing function of the size of the plateau.

In fact, this is somewhat also the dual assertion of that given in claim A.2. When the size of the plateau increases, that of the global basin decreases.

CLAIM A.7.– The difficulty is a decreasing function of the value of the plateau.

Intuitively, it can be said that this is simply a variant of claim A.3, but which should still be verified. Landscapes such as the one in Figure A.15 are then used. The result is visible in Figure A.16. The same type of decrease is indeed still present and effort values are moreover very similar.

CLAIM A.8.– The contribution to the difficulty of a plateau varies little according to its distance to the global minimum.

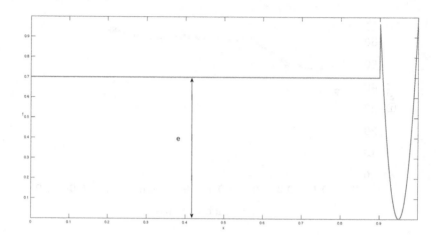

Figure A.15. *A plateau, a basin. We vary the value e of the plateau*

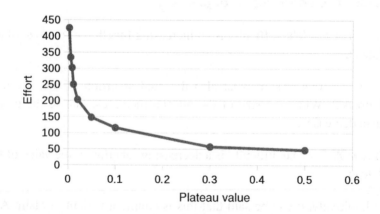

Figure A.16. *Effort versus plateau value*

By "distance", we establish here somewhat arbitrarily that it is the distance from the center (gravity center) of the plateau domain. By generating a series of landscapes similar to those of Figure A.17, the curve of effort of Figure A.18 is obtained. Again, it can be observed that distance has little impact regarding the contribution to the difficulty of the landscape.

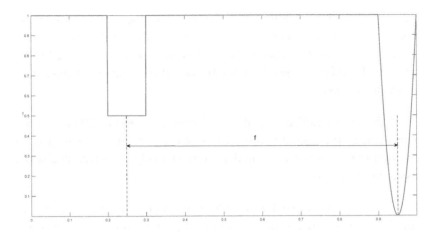

Figure A.17. *Moving plateau. We vary the distance* f

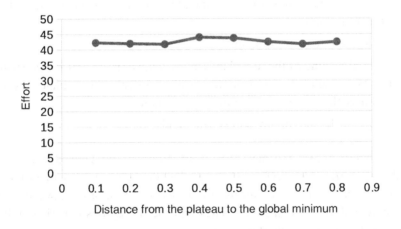

Figure A.18. *Effort versus distance from the plateau to the global minimum*

A.8.3. *Combining the rules*

Naturally, as has been seen for claim A.6, the experiments above are slightly deceptive insofar as the various behaviors are actually not independent. For example, "moving" a plateau generally modifies the size of a number of adjacent domains. It is therefore necessary to combine these behaviors in a unique model that reflects their interactions. On the contrary, one also does not seek to faithfully recover the difficulty levels (namely the effort values) but only their ordering relation.

If the model indicates that a landscape A is more difficult than a landscape B, then, ideally, this should be experimentally confirmed for the optimizers of the class under study (namely iterative, stochastic, assuming that NisB holds).

Let us try a simple formalization by neglecting the influence of the distance and by not distinguishing the contributions of basins and plateaus, due to the fact that they are similar. It is assumed that domains are numbered from 1 to m. We define:

– i^* the rank in the domain of the global minimum and f_{i^*} the value of this minimum;

– s_i the size of the domain i;

– f_i the value of the local landscape on the domain i. If it is a basin, then the value of the local minimum is considered. For a plateau, it is obviously the value at any point of its domain;

– f_{max} the maximum value of the landscape.

Therefrom, several measures of difficulty can be devised following the aforementioned rules. The one defined below seems to provide good consistency (in terms of ordering relation) between the theoretical values that it calculates and the difficulties experimentally estimated with various algorithms.

A.8.3.1. *Measure δ_0*

Let

$$\delta = \frac{1}{s_{i^*}} + \sum_{i \neq i^*} s_i \frac{f_{max} - f_{i^*}}{f_i - f_{i^*}} \qquad \text{[A.12]}$$

To then have a normalized measure on $I = [0, 1]$, it is sufficient to note that δ is in $\mathbb{R}_+^* =]0, \infty[$ and to utilize any strictly increasing function of $\mathbb{R}_+^*$ in I, for example, $1 - \frac{1}{\sqrt{\delta} + \frac{\delta_{uni}}{1 - \delta_{uni}}}$ or $2\frac{\arctan(\delta)}{\pi}$. In the first formula, which "spreads" better values in I and thus facilitates discriminations, δ_{uni} is an arbitrary value of difficulty for a unimodal landscape in dimension 1.

With $\delta_{uni} = \frac{1}{2}$, it follows that

$$\delta_0 = 1 - \frac{1}{1 + \sqrt{\delta}} \qquad\qquad \text{[A.13]}$$

A.9. Optimizer effectiveness

There are many ways to estimate the effectiveness of an iterative optimizer. None of them is absolute, because they all depend on at least two elements:

– a test case of $P = \{P_1, \ldots, P_N\}$ problems;

– the search effort, which is frequently reduced to the number E evaluations of positions in the search space.

In addition, criteria are often questionable. A discussion on this issue is presented in Clerc (2015).

Here, to simplify the presentation:

– a value ε is given (acceptability threshold) of which it is known that it is both greater than the global minimum and smaller than all local minima;

– for every problem P_i, addressed with effort E, we denote the success rate $\tau(P, E, \varepsilon)$ (abbreviated to τ_i). For a deterministic algorithm, it is 1 if the final value found is less than ε, zero otherwise. For a stochastic algorithm, it is an estimate, calculated on a large number of independent tests. In practice, we consider the *success rate versus number of tests* curve and increase the number of tests until it seems to reach a stable level.

Then, an indicator of effectiveness can be calculated as the average of success rates

$$\varphi(P, E, \varepsilon) = \frac{\sum_{i=1}^{N} \tau(P_i, E, \varepsilon)}{N} \qquad\qquad [\text{A.14}]$$

The advantage of this formula is that it highlights the fact that effectiveness is a very relative concept. Its value can be easily manipulated by tweaking the test case, the search effort or the acceptability threshold. The first two points are studied in Clerc (2015). We now quickly explain how modifying the threshold of acceptability can radically change the conclusion when comparing optimizers.

For a given problem, a given effort and two stochastic optimizers (the most general case) O_1 and O_2, the success rate can be estimated for different acceptability threshold values and the two corresponding curves can be plotted (see Figure A.19). If they do not intersect, then an assertion such as "O_1 is better than O_2" can be considered as entirely true. However, it is not uncommon that they share at least an intersection point, namely at the threshold value ε^*, and give a success rate τ^*. In this case, the assertion is undecidable or, more specifically, depends on users' expectations. If they really want results lower than ε^*, then O_1 is preferable, but if they are less demanding and allow, to a certain extent, for results larger than ε^*, then in that case, O_2 is the best choice.

A.10. Explo2+

The pseudo-code for the Explo2 algorithm is given in Chapter 8. It should be recalled that this algorithm was written just to use as close as possible the formal definitions of exploitation and exploration (see Chapter 7) in order to clearly highlight the influence of their balance ratio. As a result, it is not very efficient, despite being moreover acceptable, at least for small problems, its computational time increasing significantly with the dimension.

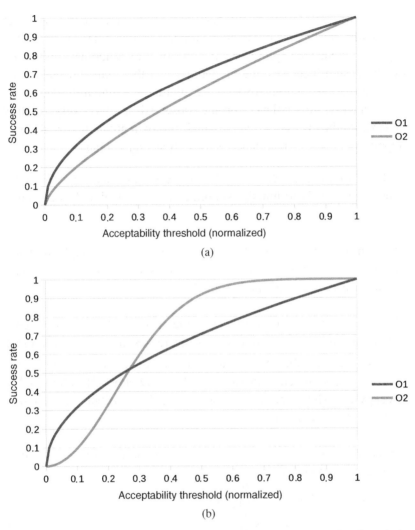

Figure A.19. *Success rate versus acceptability threshold. Cumulative distributions for two optimizers and with a given problem. (a) Optimizer O_1 is better than O_2. (b) O_1 is better than O_2, if users are looking for a result smaller than 0.265. If they are less demanding, O_2 is preferable. For a color version of this image, see www.iste.co.uk/clerc/iterative.zip*

Nevertheless, let us show here that it is easy to modify it to drastically decrease computation time, for example by replacing exploration outside exploitation domains by pure random sampling. As the dimension increases, the probability that the point supposed to be of exploration is in fact of exploitation, actually decreases. Consequently, the balance profile observed is only very slightly underneath the one requested — which is only a guide, not an absolute imperative — and performance is then often very similar.

Therefore, in practice, if we choose Explo2 as a starting point to try to build a faster algorithm, this simplification is undoubtedly a good first step.

In Explo2+, if, in order to explore, a position is simply drawn randomly, it is possible that, in fact, it is inside an exploitation domain. But, with what probability?

If N points have been sampled in the space $[0, 1]^D$, the average radius ρ of exploitation domains decreases as $\frac{1}{2N^{\frac{1}{D}}}$. If these domains are D-cubes, this radius is in fact their semi-latus and, in the worst case (evenly distributed), the N D-cubes of volume ρ^N occupy the whole space. Even with irregular distribution, the risk can thus be quite high.

If these domains are D-spheres, the volume occupied by the set of operation domains is

$$V_{exploit}(D) \leq N \frac{2\pi^{\frac{D+1}{2}}}{\Gamma\left(\frac{D+1}{2}\right)} \rho^D$$

$$\leq \frac{\pi^{\frac{D+1}{2}}}{2^{D-1}\Gamma\left(\frac{D+1}{2}\right)}$$

This volume is also the probability of drawing a point inside an exploitation domain. Note that this probability is independent of N, due to the fact that the larger N is, the smaller ρ is. The figure below shows that, even if it reaches a maximum for $D = 6$, it remains negligible, at least of the order of 3×10^{-5} and, in addition, rapidly tending to zero when D increases.

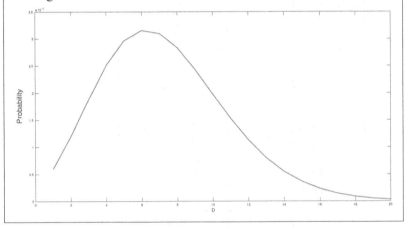

Box A.1. *The probability of exploiting by mistake*

Let us complete the summary comparison in Table 8.1 of Chapter 8, by adding the results of Explo2+ and indicating medians (see Table A.2). For Explo2+, the best results are obtained with $\alpha = 0$ (exploitation is achieved only around the best current position). Even so, it can be seen that for the Pressured Vessel problem the algorithm is significantly worse than "pure" Explo2. However, on my computer, it is also about 34 times faster. If, for the user, computational time is an important criterion, such reduction may allow us to consider sacrificing some performance.

Problem	D	Budget	APS minimum (median)	APS proba-bility	Explo2 profile 6 $\alpha = 0.1$ minimum (median)	Explo2 profile 6 $\alpha = 0.1$ proba-bility	Explo2+ profile 6 $\alpha = 0$ minimum (median)	Explo2+ profile 6 $\alpha = 0$ proba-bility
CEC 2011. The Bifunctional Catalyst Blend Optimal Control Problem	1	24,00	1.151489×10^{-5}* (1.151489×10^{-5})	1	ditto ditto	1	ditto ditto	1
Gear Train	4	4,900	2.700857×10^{-12}* (9.75×10^{-10})	0.03	ditto (6.19×10^{-9})	0.01	ditto (2.72×10^{-8})	0.02
Pressure Vessel	4	4,900	6059.83 (6413.4)	0.01	7084.80 (31207)	0.01	10,908.75 (38,272)	0.01
CEC 2011. Transmission Network Expansion Planning (TNEP) Problem	7	6,400	220* (220)	1	ditto (261.5)	0.04	ditto (262)	0.03

Table A.2. Summary comparison of APS, Explo2 and Explo2+. The minimum probability is estimated over 100 runs. An asterisk indicates that it is the global minimum. D is the problem dimension and the budget is the number of evaluations for every run

A.11. Greedy

The pseudocode of the greedy algorithm, of the "greedy" type as its name might suggest, is given in Algorithm A.1.

The algorithm is deliberately very rudimentary. The only small sophistication lies in the searching process "around" a position. It resorts to a bell-type probabilistic distribution with finite support, such as the one in Figure A.20.

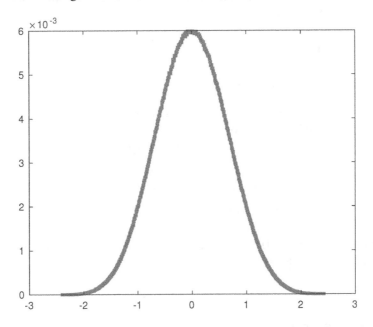

Figure A.20. *Bell-shaped probabilistic distribution*

Main program

Uniform random initialization of N positions $\Rightarrow$
$N_{eval} = N$.
Store the best location x^*.
While $N_{eval} < Budget$

    -sample a point x "around x^*"
    -if x is better than x^*, take it as the new x^*
    $N_{eval} \rightarrow N_{eval} + 1$

Procedure "around x^*"

For every coordinate x_d^*

    - apply a perturbation ("bell-like"
      distribution)

$$x_d = x_d^* + \frac{1}{2N} \frac{\sum_{i=1}^{5} U(0,1)}{5}$$

    - confine in the normalized search space

$$x_d \rightarrow \min(1, \max(0, x_d))$$

NOTE.– Each $U(0,1)$ is a realization of the uniform random
distribution on $[0,1]$.

Algorithm A.1. *A simple greedy*

A.12. Source codes

All codes given here are in the Matlab® language (2017).

A.12.1. *Random sampling in a D-sphere*

Sampling may be uniform or not. In practice, in the case of
exploitation, it is often advantageous that it is not, but on the contrary,
that it is denser around the center. In this version, if equal to 1, the
option parameter indicates to transform the sphere inside its described
cube into a sphere with the same volume of the said cube. This is to

compensate the tendency towards zero, when the dimension increases, of the ratio of the inscribed sphere/cube volumes.

```
function [x] = alea_sphere(D, radius,density)
%* ******* Random point in a hypersphere ********
% Maurice.Clerc@WriteMe.com
% Last update: 2017-11
% Put a random point inside the hypersphere S(0,
radius)
% density=1 => Uniform distribution
% <1 => less dense around the center
% >1 => denser around the center
option=0; % 1 => Increase the radius.
if ~exist('density') density=1; end
if option==1 rEquiv=2*(gamma(D/2+1)^(1/D))/sqrt(pi);
end
% --------- Step 1. Direction
l = 0;
for j=1:1:D
x(j) = randn;
l = l + x(j)*x(j);
end
l=sqrt(l);
% --------- Step 2. Random radius
r=rand;
if option==1
r=r*rEquiv;
end
alpha=density/D;
r=r^alpha;
x= r*radius*x/l;
end
```

A.12.2. SunnySpell: *potential function*

When a given number of points have already been sampled, the minimum of this function gives us a point of exploration, the idea being that it must be "far" from all others. In practice, the search for this minimum does not have to be accurate; a single low-budget run of any decent optimizer execution is generally enough.

```
function fit=sunnyspell(sunny,x, b)
% SunnySpell potential
% suggested value for b: 0.1
% sunny = set of fixed points (usually sampled by
an optimiser)
% x = point to evaluate
[N,D]=size(sunny);
if ~exist('b') b=0.1; end
% Repulsion N points
attr=Inf;
for n=1:N
a=norm(x-sunny(n,:));
attr=min(a^b,attr);
end
r1=1/attr;
% Repulsion "sides"
attr=Inf;
for d=1:D
attr=min(attr,x(d)^b);
attr=min(attr,(1-x(d))^b);
end
r2=1/attr;
% To maximise isolation
fit=r1+r2;
end
```

A.12.3. *Valuex: evaluation for a LandGener landscape*

When the domains of the landscape are D-triangles, its description is a text file that has to be read and processed. For regular landscapes on D-squares, one more simply utilizes local paraboloids that are supposed to have been previously defined (see section A.12.4).

```
function f=valuex(xx, x,middle,triangle, structure,
    smooth,domainRank)
%{
Used for a function defined by a .txt file that
    contains
x, middle, triangle and structure (see LandGener)
OR
for a regular function (multiparaboloid) defined on
    D-squares
%}
global regular
global nbParabD localMinF sizeA sameMinF indParab
persistent DA % Just to not to have to recompute it
    every time
if regular
f=multiparaboloid(xx,nbParabD,localMinF, sizeA,
    sameMinF,indParab)
return f;
end
[nbDom,D1]=size(triangle);
D=D1-1;
polynom3=false ; % General case
% Just for D=1. And it implies the "middle" position
% is not used, and replaced by (x_i-x_(i+1))/2
% Note; if you set here to false, it works, and
    with the real "middle"
% position, but the generated landscape is piece-
    wise linear
DD=D;
if isempty(DA)
DA=nan(nbDom,D+2);
end
switch DD
case 1 % In this case we use a polynomial of degree 3,
% just for a nice look
if ~exist('domainRank')
```

```
% Finds the domain ins in which xx is
isInside=false;
for ins=1:nbDom
xt=x(triangle(ins,:),:);
x1=xt(1);
x2=xt(2);
if (xx-x1)*(xx-x2)<=0
isInside=true;
break;
end
end
if ~isInside
[ind,dxx]=dsearchn(x,xx); % Nearest point, distance
[tr,v]=find(triangle(:,:)==ind); % Which triangle
    and which vertex?
f=structure(tr(1),1+v); % Value of the vertex
f=f+dxx; % Slope
return
end
else
% if domainRank is given
ins=domainRank;
xt=x(triangle(ins,:),:);
x1=xt(1);
x2=xt(2);
end
if structure(ins,1)==0 % Plateau
f=structure(ins,2);
else
x3=(x1+x2)/2;
f1=structure(ins,2);
f2=structure(ins,3);
f3=structure(ins,4);
if polynom3
if isnan(DA(ins,1))
F=[f1, f2, f3, 0]';
M=[
```

```
x1^3 x1^2 x1 1;
x2^3 x2^2 x2 1;
x3^3 x3^2 x3 1;
3*x3^2 2*x3 1 0
];
DA(ins,1:4)=linsolve(M,F);
end % if isnan(DA(ins,1))
f=DA(ins,1)*xx^3 + DA(ins,2)*xx^2 + DA(ins,3)*xx +
   DA(ins,4);
else % Two semi-parabolas
x3m=middle(ins);
if xx<=x3m
coeff=(f1-f3)/(x1-x3m)^2;
f=coeff*(xx-x3m)^2+f3;
else
coeff=(f2-f3)/(x2-x3m)^2;
f=coeff*(xx-x3m)^2+f3;
end
end % if polynom3
end % if plateau
otherwise % For D>1
% Finds the domain ins in which x is
if ~exist('domainRank')
for ins=1:nbDom
xt=x(triangle(ins,:),:);
[isInside,~]=inside(xx,xt);
if isInside
break;
end
end
if ~isInside
[ind,dxx]=dsearchn(x,xx); % Nearest point, distance
[tr,v]=find(triangle==ind(1)); % Which triangle
   and which vertex?
f=structure(tr(1),1+v(1)); % Value of the vertex
f=f+dxx; % Slope
return
```

```
end
else % if domainRank is given
ins=domainRank;
xt=x(triangle(ins,:),:);
end
% At this point we know in which domain xx is
if structure(ins,1)==0 % If plateau, no need to
    compute anything
f=structure(ins,2);
else % For a basin, we build a nice unimodal local
    landscape
% Builds and solves a linear system
xt=[xt;middle(ins,:)]; % Add the "middle" point
if isnan(DA(ins,1))
F=structure(ins,2:D+3)';
% Matrice M for interpolation
M=zeros(D+2,D+2);
% For each vertice, computes the distances
% to all the others and to the middle
for d1=1:D+1
for d2=d1+1:D+2
M(d1,d2)=norm(xt(d1,:)-xt(d2,:));
M(d1,d2)=M(d1,d2)^smooth;
M(d2,d1)=M(d1,d2);
end
end
try
DA(ins,:)=linsolve(M,F);
catch
fprintf('\nvalue. ins=%i',ins)
fprintf('\n size of DA:'); disp(size(DA))
fprintf('\n F'); disp(F)
fprintf('\nM'); disp(M)
%DA(ins,:)=linsolve(M,F);
end
end % if l==0 || l>ins
```

```
% Distances from the position to the vertices and
    to the "middle"
for d=1:D+2
dd(d)=norm(xx-xt(d,:));
dd(d)=dd(d)^smooth;
end
%{
Evaluates f as a linear combination of these
    distances.
The coefficients are kept in DA for the next calls.
They have been defined above to be sure of the local
    landscape
contains the D+1 vertices of the domain, and also
    its "middle"
%}
try
f=DA(ins,:)*dd';
catch
fprintf('\nvalue. The position is inside the domain
    %i',ins);
fprintf('\n There are %i domains ', nbDom);
fprintf('\n but there is an error. Here is the size
    of DA:');
disp(size(DA))
error(' ')
end
end % if structure(i,1)==0
end
%=================================
function fit=multiparaboloid(x,nbParabD,localMinF,
    sizeA, sameMinF,...
indParab)
% Evaluate the position x
% The landscape has been defined by multiparaboloid
    Define
[D,~]=size(x);
dxParabD=1/nbParabD;
```

```
for d=1:D % Find the paraboloid and its middle
r(d)=floor(x(d)*nbParabD);
mind=dxParabD*r(d);
maxd=mind+dxParabD;
m(d)=0.5*(mind+maxd);
end
r1=min(r+1,nbParabD);
fit=0;
for d=1:D
fit=fit+(x(d)-m(d))^2;
end
fit=fit/(D*(dxParabD/2)^2); % Normalize to 1
if sameMinF>0
if ~isequal(indParab,r1) % If not global minimum
    domain
fit=sameMinF+(1-sameMinF)*fit; % Same local minima
end
else
for n=1: length(localMinF) % Modify some local minima
[out{1:D}]=ind2sub(sizeA,n);
ind=cell2mat(out);
if isequal(ind,r1)
lmf=localMinF(n);
fit=lmf+(1-lmf)*fit;
break;
end
end
end
end
```

A.12.4. *Multiparaboloid generation*

This module is included in LandGener, but can also be directly employed, by then making use of the module multiparaboloid (section A.12.3) at every position evaluation.

```
function [LB,UB]=multiparaboloidDefine(D)
global nbParabD localMinF sizeA sameMinF indParab
```

```
rng(123456789); % Initialize the RNG for
    reproducible landscape
% Modify it to have another landscape.
%------------------------------------------------
LB=zeros(1,D);
UB=ones(1,D);
nbParabD=5; % Number of intervals on each dimension
% => nbParabD^D domains (D-cubes)
sameMinF=0; % Common value of the local minima, if
    >0
% if <=0, then random values (see localMinF)
plateauRate=0; %Â Useful only if sameMinF==0
npd=nbParabD^D;
if sameMinF<=0
localMinF=0.1 +0.9*rand(1,npd); % Values of the
    minima.
% Replace some paraboloids by a plateau
nbPlateau=plateauRate*npd;
for n=1:nbPlateau
localMinF(randi(npd))=1;
end
end
% Define the global minimum position (value zero)
globMin=randi(npd);
localMinF(globMin)=0;
sizeA=[]; for d=1:D sizeA=[sizeA nbParabD]; end;
% Display its position
[out{1:D}]=ind2sub(sizeA,globMin);
indParab=cell2mat(out);
fprintf('\n The theoretical minimum zero is on \n');
disp((indParab-0.5)/nbParabD)
% delta0 difficulty
delta0=multiparaboloidDelta0(nbParabD,local
    MinF, sizeA, sameMinF,
... globMin);
end
%------------------------------------------------
```

```
function delta0=multiparaboloidDelta0(nbParabD,
   localMinF, sizeA,...
     sameMinF,globMin)
% Evaluate the delta0 difficulty
% The landscape has been defined by multiparaboloid
   Define
D=length(sizeA);
dxParabD=1/nbParabD;
domainSize=dxParabD^D; % All D-squares have the same
   size
nbDom=length(localMinF);
delta=0;
for n=1:nbDom
  if n==globMin continue; end
  delta=delta+1/localMinF(n);
end
delta=1/domainSize+domainSize*delta;
% Normalisation
 delta0=1-1/(sqrt(delta)+1);
 fprintf('\ndelta0 difficulty: %f \n',delta0);
end
```

To test and display the landscape obtained, launch, for example, multiparaboloidTest(2).

```
function multiparaboloidTest(D)
% Just for dimension D=1 or 2
global nbParabD localMinF sizeA sameMinF indParab
multiparaboloidDefine(D); % See the hard coded
   parameters in it
% Plot
switch D
case 1
u(1)=0;
n=1000;
du=1/(n-1);
```

```
for i=2:n
u(i)=u(i-1)+du;
end
f=[];
for i=1:n
f(i)=multiparaboloid(u(i),nbParabD,localMinF, sizeA,
   sameMinF,...
indParab) ;
end
h=figure('NumberTitle','off');
hp=plot(u,f, 'LineWidth',2);
axis([min(u) max(u) min(f) max(f)+2*eps]);
xlabel('x'); ylabel('f')
set(get(gca,'YLabel'),'Rotation',0);
case 2
n=50;
u=linspace(0,1,n);
y=u;
h = waitbar(0,'I prepare the plot. Please wait...');
for i=1:n
waitbar(i/n)
for j=1:n
f(i,j)=multiparaboloid([u(i);y(j)],nbParabD,local
   MinF, sizeA,...
sameMinF,indParab) ;
%fprintf('\n i %i, j %i, u %f, y %f, f %f',i,j,u(i),
   y(j),f(i,j))
end
end
figure
hs=surfc(u,y,f);
ax=gca;
ax.YAxisLocation = 'left';
xlabel('y'); ylabel('x'); % Just for easier
   comparison with the
```

```
axis ij; % following figure (the domains)
view(-104,40);
close (h)
end
end
```

A.13. LandGener landscapes

LandGener can create two types of landscapes:

– based on D-squares and calculated by multiparaboloidDefine as stated in section A.12.4;

– based on D-triangles and described by text files. We give here only examples of deceptive functions. See section 4.2 for the explanation of the structure of such a file.

Note that the text description is redundant and could be more compact. This is intentional to allow small "manual" changes such as the introduction of discontinuity between two sub-landscapes.

A.13.1. T_1 deceptive

Dimension 1, five domains including three plateaus. Minimum 0.16360 at 0.209283.

```
5 1 6 1.0
0.000000
0.119953
0.298613
0.531127
0.999887
1.000000
0.059977
0.209283
0.414870
0.765507
```

```
0.999943
1 2
2 3
3 4
4 5
5 6
0 0.460766 0.487774 0.449341
1 0.098860 0.044785 0.016360
0 0.528205 0.528205 0.419613
1 0.488917 0.449809 0.234405
0 0.598006 0.891801 0.110574
0.209283
0.16360
```

A.13.2. T_2 *deceptive*

Dimension 1, 11 domains, minimum 0.000381 at 0.084735.

```
11 1 12 1.0
0.000000
0.063929
0.105541
0.203562
0.220626
0.272074
0.448235
0.535957
0.584396
0.596147
0.997528
1.000000
0.031964
0.084735
0.154552
0.212094
0.246350
```

```
0.360155
0.492096
0.560177
0.590272
0.796838
0.998764
1 2
2 3
3 4
4 5
5 6
6 7
7 8
8 9
9 10
10 11
11 12
1 0.830107 0.956958 0.809348
1 0.001371 0.850822 0.000381
1 0.850822 0.929169 0.794783
1 0.982783 0.783506 0.745617
1 0.783506 0.716756 0.716348
1 0.730705 0.695939 0.619109
1 0.695939 0.578710 0.506373
1 0.680959 0.475804 0.448202
1 0.797500 0.767734 0.422488
1 0.401516 0.322143 0.245990
1 0.322143 0.854437 0.073457
0.084735
0.000381
```

A.13.3. T_3 *deceptive*

Dimension 1, two domains. Minimum is 0 at 0.95. Local minimum 0.001 at 0.01.

```
2  1  3  1.0
0.000000
```

```
0.9
1.000000
0.01
0.95
1 2
2 3
1 1 1 0.001
1 1 1 0
0.95
0.0
```

A.13.4. T_4 *deceptive*

Dimension 1, 26 domains. Minimum 0.007342 at 0.042296.

```
26  1  27  1.0
0.000000
0.084591
0.124567
0.127006
0.148887
0.204610
0.250882
0.269286
0.280185
0.322766
0.400281
0.419027
0.476495
0.476833
0.498847
0.543503
0.547446
0.584616
0.603108
0.638853
0.656132
```

```
0.741631
0.803633
0.870981
0.907703
0.909062
1.000000
0.042296
0.104579
0.125787
0.137947
0.176749
0.227746
0.260084
0.274736
0.301476
0.361523
0.409654
0.447761
0.476664
0.487840
0.521175
0.545475
0.566031
0.593862
0.620981
0.647493
0.698881
0.772632
0.837307
0.889342
0.908382
0.954531
1 2
2 3
3 4
4 5
5 6
```

```
6 7
7 8
8 9
9 10
10 11
11 12
12 13
13 14
14 15
15 16
16 17
17 18
18 19
19 20
20 21
21 22
22 23
23 24
24 25
25 26
26 27
1 0.103706 0.768171 0.007342
1 0.985002 0.990867 0.899412
1 0.979618 0.934242 0.879071
1 0.943043 0.907051 0.867408
1 0.875766 0.844787 0.830191
1 0.847013 0.781639 0.781277
1 0.753869 0.898113 0.750260
1 0.850395 0.794941 0.736207
1 0.794941 0.875947 0.710559
1 0.835859 0.844370 0.652964
1 0.620402 0.865858 0.606799
1 0.865858 0.833603 0.570249
1 0.932924 0.959152 0.542527
1 0.959152 0.937711 0.531807
1 0.990758 0.787046 0.499834
1 0.536469 0.886272 0.476527
```

```
1 0.987407 0.808403 0.456810
1 0.808403 0.449917 0.430116
1 0.647242 0.999471 0.404105
1 0.473262 0.531857 0.378676
1 0.531857 0.941673 0.329386
1 0.941673 0.444190 0.258648
1 0.444190 0.311990 0.196615
1 0.165873 0.475912 0.146706
1 0.475912 0.485641 0.128443
1 0.485641 0.694623 0.084180
0.042296
0.007342
```

A.13.5. T_5 *deceptive*

Dimension 1, two domains. Minimum 0.0 at 0.95. Local minimum 0.01 at 0.01.

```
2 1 3 1.0
0.000000
0.9
1.000000
0.01
0.95
1 2
2 3
1 1 1 0.01
1 1 1 0
0.95
0.0
```

References

APS, "Adaptive Population-based Simplex", available at: http://aps-optim.info/.

Chen, J., Xin, B., Peng, Z., Dou, L., Zhang, J. (2009). Optimal contraction theorem for exploration-exploitation tradeoff in search and optimization. *IEEE Transactions on Systems, Man, and Cybernetics – Part A: Systems and Humans*, 39(3), 680–691.

Clerc, M. (2003). TRIBES – Un exemple d'optimisation par essaim particulaire sans paramètres de contrôle, in *OEP'03* (Optimisation par Essaim Particulaire), Paris, available at: http://www.particle swarm.info/oep_2003.

Clerc, M. (2005). *L'optimisation par essaims particulaires. Versions paramétriques et adaptatives*, Hermés Science-Lavoisier.

Clerc, M. (2007). When nearer is better, Technical report, Open archive, available at: https://hal.archives-ouvertes.fr/hal-00137320.

Clerc, M. (2012). Standard particle swarm optimisation, Technical report, available at: http://hal.archives-ouvertes.fr/ hal-00764996.

Clerc, M. (2014). Les essaims particulaires, in P. Siarry (ed.), *Métaheuristiques*, Eyrolles, 199–221.

Clerc, M. (2015). *Guided Randomness in Optimization*, ISTE Ltd, London and John Wiley & Sons, New York.

Conway, J.H., Guy, R.K. (1996). *The Book of Numbers*, Springer, New York. Available at: http://link.springer.com/10.1007/978-1-4612-4072-3.

Cooren, Y., Clerc, M., Siarry, P. (2008). Initialization and displacement of the particles in TRIBES, a parameter-free particle swarm optimization algorithm, in C. Cotta, M. Sevaux, K. Sörensen (eds), *Adaptive and Multilevel Metaheuristics, number 136 in 'Studies in Computational Intelligence'*, Springer Berlin Heidelberg, pp. 199–219.

Das, S., Suganthan, P.N. (2011). Problem definitions and evaluation criteria for CEC 2011 competition on testing evolutionary algorithms on real world optimization problems, Technical report.

Elsayed, S.M., Sarker, R.A., Essam, D.L. (2011a), Differential evolution with multiple strategies for solving CEC2011 real-world numerical optimization problems, in *2011 IEEE Congress of Evolutionary Computation (CEC)*, pp. 1041–1048.

Elsayed, S.M., Sarker, R.A., Essam, D.L. (2011b), GA with a new multi-parent crossover for solving IEEE-CEC2011 competition problems, in *2011 IEEE Congress of Evolutionary Computation (CEC)*.

Goldberg, D.E. (1992). Construction of high-order deceptive functions using low-order Walsh coefficients, *Annals of Mathematics and Artificial Intelligence*, 5(1), 35–47, available at: https://link.springer.com/article/10.1007/ BF01530779.

Lereuchon, J. (1622). *Selectæ Propositiones*.

Locatelli, M. (2003). A note on the Griewank test function, *Journal of Global Optimization*, 25(2), 169–174, available at: http://link.springer.com/article/10.1023/A%3A1021956306041.

MVMO. (2018). Mean-Variance Mapping Optimization, available at: https://www.uni-due.de/mvmo/.

Naudts, B., Schippers, A. (1999). A motivated definition of exploitation and exploration, Technical report.

Omran, M.G.H., Clerc, M. (2016). An adaptive population-based simplex method for continuous optimization. *International Journal of Swarm Intelligence Research*, 7(4), 22–49.

Omran, M.G.H., Clerc, M. (2017). APS 9: An improved adaptive population-based simplex method for real-world engineering optimization problems, *Applied Intelligence*, pp. 1–13, available at: https://link.springer.com/article/10.1007/s10489-017-1015-z.

Onwubolu, G.C., Babu, B.V. (2004). *New Optimization Techniques in Engineering*, Springer, Berlin, Germany.

Papadimitriou, C.H., Steiglitz, K. (1978). Some examples of difficult traveling salesman problems. *Operations Research*, 26(3), 434–443, available at: http://www.jstor.org/stable/169754.

Sandgren, E. (1990). Nonlinear integer and discrete programming in mechanical design optimization. *Journal of Mechanical Design*, 112(2), 223–229, available at: http://dx.doi.org/10.1115/1.2912596.

Shang, Y.-W., Qiu, Y.-H. (2006). A note on the extended Rosenbrock function. *Evolutionary Computation*, 14(1), 119–126.

Suganthan, P., Hansen, N., Liang, J., Deb, K., Chen, Y., Auger, A., Tiwari, S. (2005). Problem definitions and evaluation criteria for the CEC 2005 special session on real parameter optimization, Technical report, Nanyang Technological University, Singapore.

Taillard E.D. (2003). A statistical test for comparing success rates, in *Metaheuristic International Conference MIC'03*, Kyoto, Japan.

Taillard, E.D., Waelti, P., Zuber, J. (2008). Few statistical tests for proportions comparisons, *European Journal of Operational Research*, 185 (3), 136–1350.

Weber, V. (2013). Caractérisation des instances difficiles de problèmes d'optimisation NP-difficiles, PhD thesis, Université de Grenoble.

Weinberger, E. (1990). Correlated and uncorrelated fitness landscapes and how to tell the difference, *Biological Cybernetics*, 63(5), 325–336, available at: https://link.springer.com/article/10.1007/BF00202749.

Weise, T., Zapf, M., Chiong, R., Nebro, A.J. (2009). Why is optimization difficult?, in J. Kacprzyk, R. Chiong (eds), *Nature-inspired Algorithms for Optimisation*, vol. 193, Springer Berlin Heidelberg, Berlin, Heidelberg, pp. 1–50, available at: http://link.springer.com/10.1007/978-3-642-00267-0_1.

Wolpert, D.H., Macready, W.G. (1997). No free lunch theorems for optimization. *IEEE Transactions on Evolutionary Computation*, 1(1), 67–82.

Yang, X.-S., Huyck, C., Karamanoglu, M., Khan, N. (2013). True global optimality of the pressure vessel design problem: A benchmark for bio-inspired optimisation algorithms, *International Journal of Bio-inspired Computation*, 5(6), 329–335, available at: http://www.inderscienceonline.com/doi/abs/10.1504/IJBIC.2013.058910.

Zambrano-Bigiarini, M., Rojas, R., Clerc, M. (2013). Standard particle swarm optimisation 2011 at CEC-2013: A baseline for future PSO improvements, in *Congress on Evolutionary Computation (CEC)*.

Index

Other titles from

in

Computer Engineering

2018

ANDRO Mathieu
Digital Libraries and Crowdsourcing
(Digital Tools and Uses Set – Volume 5)

ARNALDI Bruno, GUITTON Pascal, MOREAU Guillaume
Virtual Reality and Augmented Reality: Myths and Realities

BERTHIER Thierry, TEBOUL Bruno
From Digital Traces to Algorithmic Projections

CARDON Alain
Beyond Artificial Intelligence: From Human Consciousness to Artificial Consciousness

HOMAYOUNI S. Mahdi, FONTES Dalila B.M.M.
Metaheuristics for Maritime Operations
(Optimization Heuristics Set – Volume 1)

JEANSOULIN Robert
JavaScript and Open Data

PIVERT Olivier
NoSQL Data Models: Trends and Challenges
(Databases and Big Data Set – Volume 1)

SEDKAOUI Soraya
Data Analytics and Big Data

SALEH Imad, AMMI Mehdi, SZONIECKY Samuel
Challenges of the Internet of Things: Technology, Use, Ethics
(Digital Tools and Uses Set – Volume 7)

SZONIECKY Samuel
Ecosystems Knowledge: Modeling and Analysis Method for Information and Communication
(Digital Tools and Uses Set – Volume 6)

2017

BENMAMMAR Badr
Concurrent, Real-Time and Distributed Programming in Java

HÉLIODORE Frédéric, NAKIB Amir, ISMAIL Boussaad, OUCHRAA Salma, SCHMITT Laurent
Metaheuristics for Intelligent Electrical Networks
(Metaheuristics Set – Volume 10)

MA Haiping, SIMON Dan
Evolutionary Computation with Biogeography-based Optimization
(Metaheuristics Set – Volume 8)

PÉTROWSKI Alain, BEN-HAMIDA Sana
Evolutionary Algorithms
(Metaheuristics Set – Volume 9)

PAI G A Vijayalakshmi
Metaheuristics for Portfolio Optimization
(Metaheuristics Set – Volume 11)

2016

BLUM Christian, FESTA Paola
Metaheuristics for String Problems in Bio-informatics
(Metaheuristics Set – Volume 6)

DEROUSSI Laurent
Metaheuristics for Logistics
(Metaheuristics Set – Volume 4)

DHAENENS Clarisse and JOURDAN Laetitia
Metaheuristics for Big Data
(Metaheuristics Set – Volume 5)

LABADIE Nacima, PRINS Christian, PRODHON Caroline
Metaheuristics for Vehicle Routing Problems
(Metaheuristics Set – Volume 3)

LEROY Laure
Eyestrain Reduction in Stereoscopy

LUTTON Evelyne, PERROT Nathalie, TONDA Albert
Evolutionary Algorithms for Food Science and Technology
(Metaheuristics Set – Volume 7)

MAGOULÈS Frédéric, ZHAO Hai-Xiang
Data Mining and Machine Learning in Building Energy Analysis

RIGO Michel
Advanced Graph Theory and Combinatorics

2015

BARBIER Franck, RECOUSSINE Jean-Luc
COBOL Software Modernization: From Principles to Implementation with the BLU AGE® Method

CHEN Ken
Performance Evaluation by Simulation and Analysis with Applications to Computer Networks

CLERC Maurice
Guided Randomness in Optimization
(Metaheuristics Set – Volume 1)

DURAND Nicolas, GIANAZZA David, GOTTELAND Jean-Baptiste,
ALLIOT Jean-Marc
Metaheuristics for Air Traffic Management
(Metaheuristics Set – Volume 2)

MAGOULÈS Frédéric, ROUX François-Xavier, HOUZEAUX Guillaume
Parallel Scientific Computing

MUNEESAWANG Paisarn, YAMMEN Suchart
Visual Inspection Technology in the Hard Disk Drive Industry

2014

BOULANGER Jean-Louis
Formal Methods Applied to Industrial Complex Systems

BOULANGER Jean-Louis
Formal Methods Applied to Complex Systems:
Implementation of the B Method

GARDI Frédéric, BENOIST Thierry, DARLAY Julien, ESTELLON Bertrand,
MEGEL Romain
Mathematical Programming Solver based on Local Search

KRICHEN Saoussen, CHAOUACHI Jouhaina
Graph-related Optimization and Decision Support Systems

LARRIEU Nicolas, VARET Antoine
Rapid Prototyping of Software for Avionics Systems: Model-oriented
Approaches for Complex Systems Certification

OUSSALAH Mourad Chabane
Software Architecture 1
Software Architecture 2

PASCHOS Vangelis Th
Combinatorial Optimization – 3-volume series, 2nd Edition
Concepts of Combinatorial Optimization – Volume 1, 2nd Edition
Problems and New Approaches – Volume 2, 2nd Edition
Applications of Combinatorial Optimization – Volume 3, 2nd Edition

QUESNEL Flavien
Scheduling of Large-scale Virtualized Infrastructures: Toward Cooperative Management

RIGO Michel
Formal Languages, Automata and Numeration Systems 1:
Introduction to Combinatorics on Words
Formal Languages, Automata and Numeration Systems 2:
Applications to Recognizability and Decidability

SAINT-DIZIER Patrick
Musical Rhetoric: Foundations and Annotation Schemes

TOUATI Sid, DE DINECHIN Benoit
Advanced Backend Optimization

2013

ANDRÉ Etienne, SOULAT Romain
The Inverse Method: Parametric Verification of Real-time Embedded Systems

BOULANGER Jean-Louis
Safety Management for Software-based Equipment

DELAHAYE Daniel, PUECHMOREL Stéphane
Modeling and Optimization of Air Traffic

FRANCOPOULO Gil
LMF — Lexical Markup Framework

GHÉDIRA Khaled
Constraint Satisfaction Problems

ROCHANGE Christine, UHRIG Sascha, SAINRAT Pascal
Time-Predictable Architectures

WAHBI Mohamed
Algorithms and Ordering Heuristics for Distributed Constraint Satisfaction Problems

ZELM Martin *et al.*
Enterprise Interoperability

2012

ARBOLEDA Hugo, ROYER Jean-Claude
Model-Driven and Software Product Line Engineering

BLANCHET Gérard, DUPOUY Bertrand
Computer Architecture

BOULANGER Jean-Louis
Industrial Use of Formal Methods: Formal Verification

BOULANGER Jean-Louis
Formal Method: Industrial Use from Model to the Code

CALVARY Gaëlle, DELOT Thierry, SÈDES Florence, TIGLI Jean-Yves
Computer Science and Ambient Intelligence

MAHOUT Vincent
Assembly Language Programming: ARM Cortex-M3 2.0: Organization, Innovation and Territory

MARLET Renaud
Program Specialization

SOTO Maria, SEVAUX Marc, ROSSI André, LAURENT Johann
Memory Allocation Problems in Embedded Systems: Optimization Methods

2011

BICHOT Charles-Edmond, SIARRY Patrick
Graph Partitioning

BOULANGER Jean-Louis
Static Analysis of Software: The Abstract Interpretation

CAFERRA Ricardo
Logic for Computer Science and Artificial Intelligence

HOMES Bernard
Fundamentals of Software Testing

KORDON Fabrice, HADDAD Serge, PAUTET Laurent, PETRUCCI Laure
Distributed Systems: Design and Algorithms

KORDON Fabrice, HADDAD Serge, PAUTET Laurent, PETRUCCI Laure
Models and Analysis in Distributed Systems

LORCA Xavier
Tree-based Graph Partitioning Constraint

TRUCHET Charlotte, ASSAYAG Gerard
Constraint Programming in Music

VICAT-BLANC PRIMET Pascale *et al.*
Computing Networks: From Cluster to Cloud Computing

2010

AUDIBERT Pierre
Mathematics for Informatics and Computer Science

BABAU Jean-Philippe *et al.*
Model Driven Engineering for Distributed Real-Time Embedded Systems 2009

BOULANGER Jean-Louis
Safety of Computer Architectures

MONMARCHE Nicolas *et al.*
Artificial Ants

PANETTO Hervé, BOUDJLIDA Nacer
Interoperability for Enterprise Software and Applications 2010

SIGAUD Olivier *et al.*
Markov Decision Processes in Artificial Intelligence

SOLNON Christine
Ant Colony Optimization and Constraint Programming

AUBRUN Christophe, SIMON Daniel, SONG Ye-Qiong *et al.*
Co-design Approaches for Dependable Networked Control Systems

2009

FOURNIER Jean-Claude
Graph Theory and Applications

GUEDON Jeanpierre
The Mojette Transform / Theory and Applications

JARD Claude, ROUX Olivier
Communicating Embedded Systems / Software and Design

LECOUTRE Christophe
Constraint Networks / Targeting Simplicity for Techniques and Algorithms

2008

BANÂTRE Michel, MARRÓN Pedro José, OLLERO Hannibal, WOLITZ Adam
Cooperating Embedded Systems and Wireless Sensor Networks

MERZ Stephan, NAVET Nicolas
Modeling and Verification of Real-time Systems

PASCHOS Vangelis Th
Combinatorial Optimization and Theoretical Computer Science: Interfaces and Perspectives

WALDNER Jean-Baptiste
Nanocomputers and Swarm Intelligence

2007

BENHAMOU Frédéric, JUSSIEN Narendra, O'SULLIVAN Barry
Trends in Constraint Programming

JUSSIEN Narendra
A TO Z OF SUDOKU

2006

BABAU Jean-Philippe *et al.*
From MDD Concepts to Experiments and Illustrations – DRES 2006

HABRIAS Henri, FRAPPIER Marc
Software Specification Methods

MURAT Cecile, PASCHOS Vangelis Th
Probabilistic Combinatorial Optimization on Graphs

PANETTO Hervé, BOUDJLIDA Nacer
Interoperability for Enterprise Software and Applications 2006 / IFAC-IFIP I-ESA'2006

2005

GÉRARD Sébastien *et al.*
Model Driven Engineering for Distributed Real Time Embedded Systems

PANETTO Hervé
Interoperability of Enterprise Software and Applications 2005

Printed and bound by CPI Group (UK) Ltd, Croydon, CR0 4YY